"One way you know Priscilla Shirer can discern the voice of God is how powerfully she proclaims it. God is all over this young woman. I know of no stronger, clearer voice for our ailing culture. When Christ speaks through her, we do well to sit up straight and listen."

—BETH MOORE, AUTHOR AND SPEAKER

"Learning to discern the voice of God can be something many believers struggle to understand. They worry about missing God's voice, or not hearing Him at all. Priscilla's study takes this very important spiritual discipline and makes it simple without making it commonplace. We highly recommend this as a discipleship tool. It has made a tremendous impact on the women of our church."

—PASTOR STOVALL AND KERRI WEEMS
CELEBRATION CHURCH, JACKSONVILLE, FL

"Priscilla digs deep into Scripture and pulls out life-changing nuggets that bring people to a whole new level of understanding God's Word and hearing His voice. Who wouldn't want to hear what our Creator wants to say to us? Now we can know how to recognize it."

—PAM CASE, DIRECTOR OF LIFEWAY WOMEN

"This is a powerful, biblical book that really helps people understand clearly how to discern the voice of God in His Word and through His Spirit. I have seen *Discerning the Voice of God* impact many lives as we've studied it together. It is a life-changing book!"

—ELLEN OLFORD, DIRECTOR OF WOMEN'S MINISTRIES,
CENTRAL CHURCH, MEMPHIS, TN

DISCERNING THE VOICE OF GOD

HOW TO RECOGNIZE WHEN GOD IS SPEAKING

Revised & Updated Edition

PRISCILLA SHIRER

MOODY PUBLISHERS

CHICAGO

Editor of 2012 edition: Pam Pugh
Interior design: Ragont Design
Cover design: Design by Julia Ryan
Cover image provided by Going Beyond Ministries

All emphases in Scripture have been added by the author.

Library of Congress Cataloging-in-Publication Data

Shirer, Priscilla Evans.
    Discerning the voice of God : how to recognize when God is speaking / Priscilla Shirer. — Rev. and updated version.
        p. cm.
    ISBN 978-0-8024-5012-8
    1. God (Christianity)—Knowableness. 2. Spirituality. 3. Spiritual life—Christianity.
    4. Listening—Religious aspects—Christianity. I. Title.
    BT103.S445 2012
    231.7-dc23

                                                                                        2011023264

Moody Publishers is committed to caring wisely for God's creation and uses recycled paper whenever possible. The paper in this book consists of 10 percent post-consumer waste.

We hope you enjoy this book from Moody Publishers. Our goal is to provide high-quality, thought-provoking books and products that connect truth to your real needs and challenges. For more information on other books and products written and produced from a biblical perspective, go to www.moodypublishers.com or write to:

Moody Publishers
820 N. LaSalle Boulevard
Chicago, IL 60610

1 3 5 7 9 10 8 6 4 2

Printed in the United States of America

Jerry, this book *is still* dedicated to you.
Thank you for being an example of someone who longs to hear Him,
takes the time to hear Him, and encourages me to do the same.

CONTENTS

BETWEEN
FRIENDS

I have called you friends . . .

John 15:15

*T*here are acquaintances, and then there are friends.

Acquaintances recognize you when they see you, ask about the ages of your children, wonder when's the last time you heard from someone you both used to know.

"Take care. Nice to see you."

But friends—get two friends together for ten minutes, and they're into each other's lives, not just their Christmas letters. They're connecting by heart, not just by a hug or a handshake.

And that's how I feel right now, connecting with you through the pages of this book—like friends. Perhaps you were here with me before, several years ago, when I first put this message down on paper, or you've gone through the six-week Bible study *Discerning the Voice of God*. And now, we have a chance to catch up and expand on what we've learned since.

If this is our first time to meet up like this, then I'm glad to have you as a new friend, because we have a hunger to hear from God that unites us in spirit. Probably one that each of us would freely admit some frustration over, but in the end, something we know we simply cannot live without.

And thank God, we don't have to.

Perhaps, like me, you've spent far too many years of your life not hearing or at least not recognizing His voice. You've read in the Bible about people to whom He spoke. You've heard from believers today who talk about how God has spoken to them. But maybe only rarely, if ever, would you say that you've experienced this kind of connection with Him yourself.

I can completely relate to that. I know exactly what it's like to hear nothing but silence after I've prayed and prayed about something, or to be so confused by flying thoughts and voices that I couldn't pick God's voice out of the crowd. I know the kinds of feelings and attitudes that go along with not really expecting Him to show up and leave directions.

Truly, we get one another's questions about discerning the voice of God.

But even though I've brought a lot of stubbornness and impatience to the Lord to work with, I can sit here today and testify to you—"by the mercies of God"—that He's brought me a long, long way. Through His long-suffering and steadfastness, He has invited me in to know Him better. And the more intimate I've become with Him, the more acquainted I've become with His voice. He has proven Himself to me because He loves proving His Word true—to all His children.

To you.

Therefore, with all the confidence one person can possess, I can assure you today that God does speak. I'm learning that if my spiritual ears are open, the same voice that called me into His marvelous light will speak into my daily life.

The Bible declares that God is the same "yesterday and today and forever" (Hebrews 13:8)—meaning the same God who spoke with the prophets of old also speaks with His saints today. The Old Testament says that what distinguished the faith of the Israelites from all others was that they "heard the voice of God" (Deuteronomy 4:33). The apostle Paul, writing in the New Testament, reminds us that the difference between the relationship we have with the one true God and the relationship pagans have with their idols is that their gods are silent (see 1 Corinthians 12:2).

This conversational nature of our relationship with the Almighty makes our faith unique. It isn't based on rules or regulations, on rugged pilgrimages to make, or sacred rivers to bathe in. The foundation of our faith is on sweet fellowship with God, who clearly, biblically, wants our relationship with Him to be both intimate and interactive.

I mean, come on, do you really think He loved you enough to die for you, but not enough to talk to you?

When Jesus walked the earth, He willingly revealed Himself to everyone around Him, knowing full well that many if not most would reject Him. Why then would He not desire deeply to speak to us—we who have received Him by faith through His mercy and grace? He *desires* to speak to us. In fact, He places a high priority on this because it's so crucial to the kind of relationship He wants to have with us.

And so, knowing this, we can't help but ask . . .

- Then why don't we hear Him?
- What keeps us from recognizing Him?
- How can we know when He is speaking?

That's what *Discerning the Voice of God* is all about. My goal in this book is to come alongside you, just as others have (and continue to) come alongside me, sharing what I have learned and what each of us can grow to experience in seeking to hear from the Lord.

But I want to be sure you hear me when I use the word "grow," because that's what we're doing here. We're growing. Nobody has all of this figured out, no matter how 100 percent foolproof people claim their knowledge to be. Even by the time we get all the way through this book together, we will still be more than capable of getting our fallen selves in the way of what we truly want from our walk with the Lord. But because He loves us so much, He will allow even our errors and flaws to be good teachers for the future as we keep practicing and developing under His master instruction.

As we grow.

When I first started jogging, for example, I couldn't make it halfway around the block without heaving and sputtering and finally running out of pep. Yet as discouraging as this was to my goals for better fitness, I couldn't help noticing that the attempt itself was doing something positive in me.

My body was responding to the workouts. Even though I was still doing more walking than running as I tried to complete the circuit back home, I was starting to see little-by-little improvement each day. Pitiful though it may have looked to anyone snickering at me from the neighborhood windows, and slow as it may have been while I waited for my running ability to kick in, something was happening. My body was changing and my endurance was increasing even while I was learning. The growing process is not a waste. There are benefits every small step of the way.

And thank the Lord for that! This is precisely why I've included so many personal stories in this work. I want you to see what a journey this has been for me—a journey that I've neither begun nor finished simply by reading a book or taking a course, but rather through the patient work that the Lord has done (and is still doing) in my own life in very practical ways. When I've made mistakes, missed hearing Him, or become impatient waiting for His direction, I've often felt like the journey may not have been worth it and that I'll never get this right. But I hope these very personal experiences of mine will show you how each step with Him has helped me see more clearly than before. I also pray that you'll discover how your own adventure with God is designed to do the same—build one valuable lesson on top of another as He leads you ever closer to Him.

I know how easy it can be to give up, how discouraging it can be when you don't feel like God has any interest in talking to you and revealing His will. There's a lot working against you. From the Enemy's deceptions to your own fatigue and weakness, this whole thing can seem like an impossible search. But this book hasn't caught your eye by accident. God is speaking even now, stirring in you again a desire and expectancy for His voice. And no matter where you're starting from, you can start to grow again. To grow closer. To hear Him.

What I'm about to show you are not just general guidelines, as effective as they can be. Some guidelines help us learn to hear from God. But the important thing to remember is that the only reason they "work" is because *God* is speaking—not because *we've* pushed the right buttons or lined up the pieces in the proper order. God speaks because He loves you. And apart from a relationship with Him, no amount of effort and trying can stir one whisper from the heavens. This is *His* work. *His* desire. All He asks is your receptive heart.

So as we get ready to dig in, let's say a prayer that God will bless what He's about to give us, and that He'll open our hearts, certain beyond a doubt that we'll hear from His Word and His Spirit.

Let's get started.

Priscilla

Part One

REALIZE THE WAY HE SPEAKS

IF YOU'RE LISTENING *Chapter One*

*As you enter the house of God, keep your
ears open and your mouth shut. . . .
After all, God is in heaven, and you are
here on earth. So let your words be few.*

Ecclesiastes 5:1–2 NLT

*I*t started out as a simple lunch with an old friend. That's all it was
intended to be. I sat across from Jada, a faithful confidante I'd known
since childhood, hashing out every detail of an issue that was weighing
heavily on my mind. She's a wise woman, always has been—a very insightful person. So I knew she could give me some good counsel.

We'd managed to clear an hour from our equally crowded calendars
one weekday afternoon to visit. I suggested we meet at a nearby restaurant,
not so much to dig in as to dig deep. As soon as we had been seated, I
immediately began sharing some of the main points of my problem. Before
we even sat down at the table, and then through the server introductions,
the water glass refills, the entrée deliveries, and the dessert offerings, I barely
came up for air, rambling incessantly about every detail and nuance of the
situation.

My sweet friend nodded her head sympathetically between bites of
salad and sips of iced tea. The occasional "mm-hmm" suggested that she was

still following my long, clackety train of thought. Then, as the dishes were being cleared away and the check delivered, I leaned back in my seat and finally took a breath. I saw her glance down at her watch and tug a bit at her purse.

"So . . . what do you think I should do?" I asked, a bit impatient with her hesitating response.

"Priscilla," she answered, very kindly, gently, "I did have some things to say to you, but you never stopped talking long enough to listen."

Oh.

Nothing like those faithful "wounds of a friend" (Proverbs 27:6) to smack you square in the face with the truth. In love.

I drove home that afternoon a bit disappointed. I hadn't gotten the clarity I'd hoped for. Jada hadn't said much. But reflecting on her response to my hour-long rant, the Holy Spirit *did* say something. With piercing conviction. Hadn't I been approaching Him the same way? Talking, talking, talking, talking—praying (feels better calling it that). But mostly just talking, repeating myself, analyzing, rationalizing. Like Jada, God was reminding me, "*I do have some things to say to you, Priscilla, but you never stop talking long enough to listen.*"

And with that, I'd been schooled. I'd gotten perhaps my most profound lesson to date on hearing the voice of God, and it hit me squarely in the heart.

If I wanted to hear, I had to listen.

Creating time, space, and opportunity to hear God is paramount for those of us who desire to sense His Spirit's conviction, to receive His detailed guidance, and to discern His intimate leading. Before I could even begin to explore further instruction concerning how God speaks—or even *why* He speaks—I first had to ask myself whether or not I wanted to hear Him enough to stop doing all the talking so that I might listen.

It all starts here: if we want to be able to sense His direction, we must slow down, quiet our hearts, and listen for the way His Spirit communicates.

The more I've continued to contemplate the implications of this concept, the more I've realized that it isn't just specific to my prayer life. Rather, it provides the basis for hearing from God at all times, whether I'm on my knees in prayer or on my feet hurrying through the nuances of my daily demands.

When reading His Word, it means approaching it with an open mind and heart that's not already bogged down with my own opinions and ideas of what the text is saying. It means coming with time to meditate and to mull over its personal application.

If we're always impatient, we leave little space for God's direction to resonate in our already crowded schedules.

In the regular rhythms of life, it means being willing to wait and watch, to sense where God is moving before I hurry to make a decision. It means not having all the answers I'd like to have but not becoming frazzled by that, staying quiet and patient as He gives me what I do need to know, understanding that this "empty space"—this listening posture that makes me so jumpy and uncomfortable—is exactly the void He can fill with His divine wisdom and direction. It means being attentive to the undercurrent of His ongoing activity beneath the surface of my everyday happenings.

The lesson was becoming more and more clear: creating and allowing margin to hear God is fundamental to discerning His voice. Because in that space, we seek Him, lean into Him, and acknowledge Him in a way we might not otherwise be able to. In doing so, we get the chance to really know who we're dealing with. If we're always impatient, filling in the silent margins during prayer, in our decision making, and in every other aspect of life, we leave little space for God's powerful direction to resonate in our already crowded schedules and hearts.

So as you begin your journey through the pages of this book, and before we explore the details of how you can discern God's leading, I want you to ponder this fundamental issue of *listening*, upon which hearing God ultimately hinges. What's on your list of questions for God right now?

SHOULD I

- marry this person?

- accept this position?

- look into this opportunity?

- participate in this activity?

- consent to this agreement?

- allow this outcome?

- stop this process?

Job questions . . . cars . . . raising children . . . major purchases . . . medical decisions . . . even whose-family-to-disappoint-by-not-coming-for-Christmas issues. Some of these are temporary; some potentially life-changing. Some involve choices between good and better; others between bad and worse. But they all represent problems to handle, decisions to make. Questions.

This list could go on, couldn't it? Our lives are an ever-changing catalog of intricately woven personal inquiries that we each need divine direction to navigate accurately. So while you're thinking of your list of questions, add one to it, would ya? Those others were for God; this one is for you . . .

Have you sincerely taken time to hear, to see, to wait, to watch—to allow for the margins that would give God an opportunity to offer you that which you claim to desire so earnestly? Or have you already filled in every conceivable space with your own opinions, ideas, decisions, and actions—space that God might otherwise fill with His perfectly timed and precisioned and personal insight?

The answer to this one critical question is really where the journey of hearing God begins.

Take into your heart all My words which
I will speak to you and listen closely.
Ezekiel 3:10

Listen Up

I suspect that at least some of the reason you laid eyes on this book in the first place is because you want to get to the bottom of this often hard-to-understand concept of discerning God's voice—maybe for your general, spiritual growth, but maybe also for specific, personal reasons. You need to know some things from God in relation to an important dilemma or decision in your life, and you want to find out how to hear Him more clearly so you can understand what to do.

If what you're grappling with was simply a matter of right and wrong, it might not be so hard to deal with. I pray you already believe in the truth of Scripture and all the directives that are clearly outlined in it, so the validity of these "black and white" commands from God aren't really at issue here (even if you're not always inclined to follow them). What's on your question plate right now is most likely an "either/or" kind of thing.

One of the most common reasons why we don't hear from God is perhaps the most obvious: We're not listening.

And if forced to pick an answer right this minute, you could make just as good an argument for one option as the other. Depends on the time of day. The mood you're in. The kind of meal you just ate.

Sure, you do have the Bible to consult for guidance, but you know you can't just open it at random, taking verses out of context simply to affirm your own choices. *You genuinely want to hear from God.* You want to know whether the recent circumstances you've noticed around you are more than mere coincidence, or whether the comments you heard someone make to you might truly be a signal of God's will and direction. You want to make sure that this conviction you're feeling is not just of your own creating.

And while there are many reasons why this happens—some because of our own impatience, some because of unconfessed sin in our lives clogging the connection, some because we don't know what we're even looking for when it comes to sensing the Spirit's prompting, and some because of God's

sovereign decision to make us wait a little longer than we'd like (keep reading, we'll get to all these things)—one of the most common reasons why we
don't hear from God is perhaps the most obvious. And it's the one I want
you to consider right here at the very beginning of our journey together.
Could it be that . . .

We're not listening?

I believe the most practical way we can begin to discipline ourselves in
this area is in our prayer lives. This has been one of the most stunning revelations I've had in my journey with God on the matter of discerning His
voice. So simple, yet profound. I've learned it from folks whose walk with
the Lord I greatly admire.

When I see men and women whose relationship with God is particularly inspiring, I'm not the least bit afraid to walk right up and ask them
what they attribute it to. And without fail, each person I ask—no matter
who it is—ultimately tells me the same thing: "I deliberately carve out time
in my prayer life to be still and listen for God's voice."

They spend time with Him in prayer, listening in silence for Him to
speak. For while God does speak in other venues of life beside the quiet,
secret place of prayer, these people suggest that accurately discerning His
voice starts here. Divine conversations begin in this place and then blossom
from the richness of its soil throughout the rest of their busy day.

Once I ponder the prayer life of these believers, I realize why my own
prayers have so often been weak and powerless. I begin to understand why
there's a disconnect between the power I want in my prayer life and what
I'm experiencing. I can finally put my finger on why I don't always seem to
make out what God is saying to me or how He's directing me in a particular situation.

Simple. I haven't been listening.

And if the most godly people I know—people who I'm confident hear
from Him on a regular, ongoing basis—if these people are the ones who
spend the most time listening quietly for His voice, then I want to be that
kind of person too. One who listens to God.

How about you?

Then that's where we begin.

Deliberately listening for God's voice seems to be a lost art these days. Well, let's be honest, listening *period* is a lost art. We rarely listen to each other, much less the unseen God. Instead we've inserted a lot of noise and activity—some of it well-meaning, even religious, but nonetheless fast-paced. In fact, we think God probably wouldn't be pleased with us unless we were keeping up this level of forward progress. We think all of our bustle and busyness in the pursuit of Christian living somehow makes Him *more* likely to speak to us once He recognizes how hard we're willing to work for Him.

From that perspective, stopping to listen to Him in order to make room for His guidance sounds bland and ordinary. Too easy. Uneventful. A waste of time for people who can get as much done as we can.

Yet all this commotion of ours, far from helping us, only keeps us cloudier and more overcommitted, less able to hear from God. By letting a thousand interruptions barge in, demanding to be accommodated, we only succeed in setting ourselves up for compromise and confusion. The Enemy wins a victory every time we let our jam-packed schedules invade the sanctuary of our quiet time with God. And when we allow it to happen, we set a precedent that the rest of our lives seem to end up following.

In one case I was too busy to come to God at all. In the other I was too busy (even while I was with Him) for Him to come to me.

See if this sounds familiar . . .

In the stillness of the morning, I begin my quiet time—to those moments I purposely set aside for Bible reading, prayer, meditation, *listening*—and I lean my elbows on heaven's windowsill, eager to commune with the Lord.

But first, to satisfy my curiosity, I check to see if I've gotten any new e-mails since last night.

When I finally come back, I'm a little more distracted, a little less focused and clearheaded. Suddenly the phone rings. Caller ID beckons my eyes, and I feel compelled to pick up the receiver. The anticipation is too much. I answer it.

Oh, never mind, I'll just have my quiet time before I go to bed tonight.

Ten p.m. The kids are finally in bed, dinner dishes washed, and the bills finally paid online. I've given preference to everything else over my quiet time all day long, one thing after another. Now I'm worn out and exhausted. I plop myself under the covers, my Bible on my lap. Within five minutes I'm asleep. My good intentions go out with my night light.

The Enemy smirks.

So the next morning, I'm at it again, intent on not letting another day start without spending time with God. What happened to me yesterday *will not* happen to me again. I wake up early enough, grab a cup of tea, and get going. I spend thirty whole minutes—fifteen minutes scouring a few chapters of the Bible, and another fifteen going through the list of prayer needs I keep written in my notebook. When the time is over, I can't believe how fast it's gone. I pop up and get on with my day. I feel proud not having let the opportunity pass me by again.

But have I really done a better job than the day before? Sure, spending time with Him in some way is better than none at all. But neither opportunity allowed margin for God to fill. In one case I was too busy to come to God at all. In the other I was too busy (even while I was with Him) for Him to come to me. In neither instance did I hear from God, sense His presence, or make room for His Spirit's conviction.

Reading a verse, saying a prayer, or singing a song may help you feel better about checking "quiet time" off your to-do list, but these alone won't help you get what you're after—knowing Him more intimately, uniting with His heart, and receiving His direction for your life.

Have we become so addicted to busyness—not merely in our daily lives but while we're actually immersed in our daily devotions—that we've trained ourselves *not to hear Him?*

Carving out time in prayer to purposefully listen for God's voice—His voice and nothing else—retrains us so we can hear the Spirit's whisper and gain the ability to hear Him clearly. Stopping to listen to Him enables us to become familiar with what a sense of God's presence feels like, while enlarging our understanding of His plans for us, seeing them emerge into the light.

This doesn't mean that during our devotional times we're not allowed to open our mouths and share our hearts with God in prayer. On the contrary, we're not only *allowed* to do this but we've been *instructed* to speak up and let our "requests be made known to God" (Philippians 4:6). If we want to hear Him speak, however, we must also learn to pray without words. To listen for His voice. To seek the simplicity of stillness with Him rather than consuming all the time and space ourselves. We can't allow what *we're* saying to keep us from listening to what *He* wants to say.

Not if we want to hear the voice of God.

That's why right here in the first chapter of the book, I want us to go ahead and get very practical on this fundamental issue. Again, I believe it will set the precedent for how this plays out in the other dimensions of our walk with God. Over the years I've often heard believers say what I'm saying to you now—that we must "listen" for God if we want to hear Him speak to us. But for some reason it never occurred to me that this was a concrete discipline I could apply in any sort of practical, real-world kind of way. I didn't realize that listening wasn't just some passive, "spiritual" assignment that was part of my progressive sanctification or something.

Listening to God is a purposeful activity that we are supposed to start doing. It is the investment of time we must make in order to yield the spiritual dividends of wisdom we so desperately need. The Bible tells us to "incline" our ears toward Him (Isaiah 55:3), to "draw near to listen" (Ecclesiastes 5:1). Fifteen times in the New Testament, the Lord punctuates His point with these words: "Anyone who has ears must listen . . ." (Revelation 2:29 NLT, is one example).

So expect this discipline to require some work. If you want to become an active listener, you need to learn the art of listening as I myself am seeking to. And if you're a person like me who enjoys being up and going and doing, this can prove to be a very difficult challenge. Be ready for the fact that it takes discipline and time and probably won't happen during commercial breaks or while monitoring your friends' Twitter updates.

Now don't get me wrong. I'm as captivated by modern advances as the next gal. I'm typing right now on my Apple computer while checking an incoming message on my iPhone. I'm the first to admit that I'm grateful for these gadgets and am as dazzled by them as all of

Until we intentionally discipline ourselves to be still and listen, we'll miss most of what He's saying.

us tend to be. Nothing wrong with any of these, as long as they're not controlling us.

But each "improvement" can plunge us deeper into the abyss of busyness, squelching God's voice to a distant echo. Our prayers become mindless and hurried, scattered and incoherent. All talk. All me. All on my own time frame and agenda.

That's just not how listening happens. Really listening in prayer requires getting yourself on a whole other wavelength. You must control your body's urge to get up and move around. You must fight to keep your mind from wandering, from letting stray thoughts dictate what you choose to dwell on. You must keep your eyes from scanning the room and noticing things you need to take care of—things you'd like to get busy accomplishing right now while you're thinking of it!

Listening can be a real endeavor when you actually try doing it. But, oh, once you start to hear Him, you'll be anxious to do it again and again.

While I'm still growing and fighting my tendency toward busyness, I now look forward to every opportunity to get alone with God, Bible open, pen out, ready to concentrate. When you know He's going to speak, listening for Him ceases to be a chore and becomes a cherished delight. Exhilarating. Exciting. Hearing the voice of the Almighty has changed my humdrum Christian experience from a discipline into a passion. I no longer study the Bible merely as an instructional and theological tool (though it certainly is), but also as God's love letter to me. I eagerly look into its pages as I sit quietly before Him and listen for His voice. Sure, I don't hear a clear, direct answer to my most pressing questions every time I'm quiet before Him. There are many times when I leave with nothing more than an awareness of God's nearness and His care. But that in itself is often the answer I didn't even know I needed.

I'm in no way implying that it's impossible to hear God speak amid the regular rhythms of everyday life. On the contrary, we can, and He does. We can listen while we're exercising, clipping coupons, washing dishes, sitting in traffic, taking a shower, and doing all sorts of mundane tasks. We can be aware of His handiwork moving in natural things, making them supernatural. But until we intentionally discipline ourselves to be still and listen, to acquaint ourselves with His voice and His stirrings in our private, intimate moments with Him, we'll never hear Him consistently anywhere. We'll miss most of what He's saying.

> I close my eyes to shut out visual stimuli. . . . I close my ears by dealing authoritatively with distractions which threaten my ability to tune into God. . . . I close a series of shutters on the surface level of my life, thus holding at bay hindrances to hearing the still, small voice of God, and I release a trigger that gives deeper, inner, hidden parts of myself permission to spark to life.
>
> —Joyce Huggett

Listening in Prayer

College algebra was the worst class I've ever taken. Not only because God didn't connect the math wires in my brain, but also because my professor was a poor teacher.

It was my first year at the university, and I signed up for this core curriculum class right off the bat. Wanted to get it out of the way. I can't tell you much about my professor—what he looked like or what his name was—because honestly, I never really saw him that much. He was always in front of the class teaching, but never with any enthusiasm or eagerness. In fact, every single Monday, Wednesday, and Friday at 1:30 p.m., he'd take his position in front of the three hundred students filling the auditorium. With his back turned squarely to us, he'd face the blackboard and start teaching.

For one full hour, he talked directly into the blackboard while standing right in front of whatever he was writing down. We couldn't see anything. Could barely even make out what he was saying.

Naturally, the attention span of most of the students waned very quickly during every class period. Some of us would try to stay attentive, but we found it much more intriguing to pay closer attention to one another. And while on occasion we might be able to regurgitate what the professor was saying at any given moment, we weren't really engaged in the class. Sure, we could hear his voice, but we weren't *really* listening.

It's called passive listening. The accidental, unintentional kind. Surely you've been engaged in conversation with another person, and though you're looking into her face, though you're hearing every syllable her lips are forming, you're not really listening. It's all a bunch of words that would probably mean something if you were paying attention, but you're not really even trying to digest what she's saying.

That's us. Most of the time.

Passive listeners.

But the listening that God requires is active, intentional, and aggressive. "But if you look carefully into the perfect law that sets you free, and if you do what it says and don't forget what you heard, then God will bless you for doing it" (James 1:25 NLT).

That's why unrushed times with God are essential to hearing His voice and discerning His will. There's no formula for doing this, no absolute, sure-fire steps to follow, no lists to check off. Your relationship with the Lord is as personal as you are, and He intends to deal with you as an individual.

Yet I've found that three specific activities stand out among those believers who engage in sincere fellowship with God, enabling them to receive ongoing direction from Him. If you'll try incorporating these elements into your time with Him—in whatever way He leads you to approach them—you'll create an atmosphere more conducive to listening, a laboratory for learning how to recognize His voice and respond in obedience—*worship, prayerful listening,* and *meditation.*

Worship

Anytime God is speaking—anyplace we expect to hear His voice—worship cannot be very far away. Worship rolls out the red carpet for God's presence to invade a space. I used to think *worship* was just a word that applied to the corporate gathering together of God's people, but I began to learn from mentors that worship with others is only an overflow of our personal experience. They taught me to choose whatever genre of worship music that exalted God and caused me to do the same, and let it fill the room as a prelude to my time with God. So this became my habit, meeting with Him against the backdrop of praise music, allowing the lyrics to guide me into my worship of Him—differently than I worshiped Him yesterday, differently than I'll worship Him tomorrow.

As the songs highlight an attribute of His character, I concentrate on how I've seen it revealed in my own life, and I ascribe praise to Him for it. The point is not for me to sing (although this is a beautiful offering that pleases the Lord). The purpose is to be drawn into fellowship with Him through the music.

I saw this demonstrated in a church service once. After each song during the praise and worship time at the beginning of service, the leader, singers, and musicians just stopped and prayerfully allowed a few moments of silence. Within this interlude the congregants had time to really "hear" what they'd just sung and spend time reacting personally to how the Lord might want to use it to draw them to Himself and inspire them to offer worship to Him. It was a lovely, beautiful demonstration of how each person could do the same individually.

During this part of my personal quiet time, even if only for a few minutes, I'll often feel led to get down on my knees, or perhaps lie prostrate on the floor in a position of absolute surrender and humility before Him. As the music plays, the awareness of His presence both overwhelms and encourages me. I'm not doing much, just soaking in His presence that's infiltrating the space I've created for Him and invited Him to invade. I'm waiting while I'm worshiping. I've confessed my utter dependence on His grace and empowerment. I've acknowledged who He is—the only One worthy of my trust, the only One who can always be counted on to speak truth into my life.

Now I'm listening.

Really listening.

Prayerful Listening

My prayer time used to be a one-way conversation—all talk, all the time. I felt like every word was just hitting the ceiling and bouncing back. I felt no closer to God and certainly did not sense that any conversation had taken place between the two of us.

That's when I spotted the apostle Paul's comments about his prayer life, and its message seemed to leap off the page and jump directly into my hungry heart. He wrote about praying with his mind as well as with his spirit (see 1 Corinthians 14:15). And while his comments were directly related to the operation of spiritual gifts within the Corinthian church, there's something very instructive for us in his statement. It points toward two dimensions that should encompass our prayer lives. My own prayers used to be pretty much limited to the mental part—the "mind" portion of Paul's equation—which I'm now certain kept me from experiencing the fullness of what prayer should be. I always had my list of requests, confessions, concerns, thanksgiving, and comments that I made to the Lord. But once I'd exhausted everything that was on my mind, my prayer time was over. Paul's own example encouraged me to more fully engage God's Spirit within me while in prayer.

So I've sought to no longer neglect that element to my prayer life now, and it has begun to make all of the difference. Once I'm finished bringing my prepackaged matters to God's attention, instead of ending things right there—as though I've dutifully delivered my report to Him and can now go on about my business as usual—I don't. I resist the urge to jump to my feet just because "I'm done." Sure, *I* might be done, but . . . what if God's not? *I've* gotten a chance to talk—to share with Him what is on my mind. Why should I not at least allow Him the same courtesy? So I stop allowing what my mind is aware of to control the prayer time. I pray with my "spirit."

Rather than telling God things I already know, I invite Him to tell me things only *He* knows, things He wants to share with me by His Spirit. I allow the Holy Spirit to bring people and situations to mind that I wouldn't normally think of. Then I pray for them and ask how I might be useful in ministering to these individuals personally, since that is quite possibly why He's telling me about them in the first place.

I ask Him to "search me . . . and know my heart" (Psalm 139:23), and when I sense conviction concerning a sin I didn't even realize I was committing (which I often do), I offer it to Him in prayer, seeking forgiveness and soaking it deeply in His grace.

Perhaps He brings to mind a particular passage of Scripture, so I turn there in my Bible and start to meditate on its principles, assuming the Spirit has led me here for a reason.

Who knows what He might say to me next if all I'm doing is listening? He might even give me an important indicator of His will concerning a specific matter I'd mentioned to Him when I first sat down. "The thoughts of God no one knows except the Spirit of God" (1 Corinthians 2:11). And if I'm ever to know what His thoughts are, they won't come from my own self, my own words, my own talking. Only from listening. Listening in prayer. This is God's turn to talk, and very frequently—when given the chance—He'll do just that.

Meditation

Whenever I touch on or talk about meditation, I invariably hear from folks who think I'm trailing off into some sort of spooky mysticism, like I'm getting a little weird on them. And while I'm certainly aware of the Zen-like methods used by many in our culture to achieve a more relaxed, enlightened state of being, I'm not willing to let some pagan ritual steal a piece of my spiritual arsenal simply because it's subject to misuse.

The bottom line is this: Scripture encourages believers to meditate on God and His Word. Not to empty our minds for the purpose of focusing on "nothingness" as pagan meditation aims for, but to fill them with intentional thoughts of Him and His Word (Joshua 1:8; Psalms 1:2; 119:15, 97).

Meditation is the discipline of pondering. It's what every single one of us who has ever been in love has done. We sit and think about that person— going over every facial expression, every word he last spoke to us, every little thing we most cherish about him. This, in its simplest, most sanctified form, is what God desires. He is to be the love interest we are to focus on when we meditate (in the Christian sense of the word). It is from these times of meditation that we receive clarity as His Word becomes alive and personal by the Spirit's illumination.

As I've taken this biblical directive more seriously, I've discovered I do not need to wait for Sunday to encounter Him in deep, meaningful ways. Some of my most precious moments with Him—the ones that end up in my journal for safekeeping—happen in my secret place, sitting silently all alone in His presence, sometimes with only a single verse of Scripture, perhaps only a single word or phrase, being shared back and forth between His Spirit and mine.

I slowly and deliberately allow His words to wash over me. When I read the Scriptures, I place my own name or a personal pronoun into the verse, letting it speak directly to me. If I'm reading and meditating on a particular Bible story or event, I imagine myself in the scene. For example, if I'm reading the story of the woman caught in a scandalous web of adultery by the judgmental and conniving Pharisees (John 8), I put myself in her shoes—humiliated, ashamed, guilty, but then offered grace by Jesus before all of my accusers. Becoming part of the story in this way causes me to "experience" the passage instead of just reading about it. And then, very often, it happens—a verse will open up to me. The Spirit will uncover my eyes so I can really see its truth and its application for me in the current happenings of my life. It's a thrilling moment. Sweet. Powerful. Intimate. Individual. And . . . it's worth waiting for.

At its core, meditation is about getting to know God, because the discipline of discerning His voice really boils down to one very simple yet poignant principle: The more you *know* God, the more clearly you can *hear* God. While I meditate on a passage, I'll ask myself:

- What does this verse reveal to me about Him?
- What spiritual principle does it teach?
- Am I living in a way contrary to its truth?

- How does it relate to my present circumstances?
- How should I respond to what I'm contemplating?

Forcing myself not to fill in the silence with activity, I listen for His voice to direct me. I deal authoritatively with distraction by making a list of the stray thoughts, errands, or issues that keep presenting themselves so that I feel like I've dealt with them and can get back to the business at hand. As the Spirit brings thoughts, answers, convictions, concerns, or solutions to my mind, I record them in my journal. I consider God's goodness to me, or just the goodness of God Himself. He speaks to me in ways I would never be open to considering—ways I may never experience if I only met with Him on my way between appointments or the occasional Bible study. To hear Him, I must listen. Think. Concentrate on Him. Meditate.

> First, it is "me and Him." I come to prayer conscious of myself, my need, my desires. I pour these out to God. Second, prayer becomes "Him and me." Gradually I become more conscious of the presence of God than of myself. Then it is only "Him." God's presence arrests me, captivates me, warms me, works on me.
>
> —Stephen Verney

Voice of the Shepherd

In sharing with you the details of my typical prayer time, my hope is not that you'll copy my pattern. My only goal in describing how He speaks to me in private is to motivate you to desire personal time with Him yourself. Oh, and one more thing—to make sure you know that there is never any reason to give up hope of hearing His voice again. If you don't think He's interested in giving you direction about your specific needs and questions, be encouraged. He is waiting for you to draw near to Him so He can draw near to you.

To speak to you.

Jesus, speaking to His disciples in John 10:27, assured them—and us— of this promise: "My sheep hear My voice." No ifs. No buts. No exceptions.

No escape clauses. If you're His child—if you're one of His sheep—the certainty of God speaking to you is as sure as the chair you're sitting in.

Now the relationship between sheep and shepherd is one that's foreign to most of us, but not to Jesus' original audience. They were well aware that it was routine for many flocks of sheep to be brought together to stay the night in a common sheepfold. In the morning each shepherd would return, calling his sheep to come away with him and go out to the fields for grazing. The sheep in the fold would hear many other shepherds' voices throughout those early hours of the day, but they were trained only to respond to the voice of *their* shepherd—their *true* shepherd.

When they heard that singular, undeniable voice, it didn't matter if they were light or dark sheep. Young or old. Wide or slender. High end or budget rack. All that mattered was that they were *his* sheep. *All that mattered was who they belonged to.*

So let me interject some questions to you at this point: Who do you belong to? Is Jesus Christ your true Shepherd? Have you received Him as your Lord and Savior? Do you belong to Him?

I ask because the Bible makes plain that those who have not bowed their knee to Jesus—accepting His sacrifice on the cross for our sins and committing our lives to Him, thus receiving God's Spirit—should not expect to hear the voice of the one true God in any ongoing way. All the listening in the world cannot tune the ears of the flesh to hear the holy. "People who aren't spiritual can't receive these truths from God's Spirit. It all sounds foolish to them and they can't understand it, for only those who are spiritual can understand what the Spirit means " (1 Corinthians 2:14 NLT). The person who doesn't trust Christ as Savior is missing the one essential, necessary ingredient for interacting and communicating with Him.

However, if you have placed your faith in Jesus Christ, yet you're discouraged right now because you're struggling to discern His voice, please don't doubt your salvation. That's just what the Enemy wants you to do—belittle the faithful work of God and settle for limits in your relationship with Christ.

Remember, learning to hear God's voice is a process, a learning experience, a discipline that involves active elements like prayer, meditation, worship, and *listening*. Just as any relationship grows stronger and more intimate as you spend more time getting to know a person, so your relationship with God—your ability to discern His voice and to pick it out of the crowd—will grow keener and more developed as you spend more time with Him. Even if you've been a believer for many years, even though you may be trying as hard as humanly possible to wait for Him and patiently persevere, renew yourself to starting afresh. If you've begun to doubt that He cares enough to communicate with you anymore, if you don't see how He could still love you after all you've done, if you think you've made too big of a mess for any word of His to fix or restore the damage, open your heart to Him again today. Sit with Him. Be still before Him. Don't despair.

Matthew 6:6 promises that "your Father who sees what is done in secret"—the praying, listening, and seeking—"will reward you" with His presence, His guidance, and the gripping sound of His voice. This is a priority to Him, just as it should be to us. So make time to spend with Him. He is waiting to speak to you—to anyone who truly wants to hear Him, anyone who calls out to Him.

Anyone who listens.

Chapter Challenges

- Write down the current issues in your life that you need to discern God's will regarding. As you go through this book, use your list as a reference.

- Scale back on what you will "do" during your devotional time so you can leave room to "be" with God.

- Deal authoritatively with distractions so you can concentrate on the task of listening. When something comes to mind, write it down and then set it aside.

- Allow for and accept "God margins" in all areas of your life. Relax instead of trying to fill in every space with your own ideas, decisions, and actions.

INSIDE
INFORMATION *Chapter Two*

Do you not know that you are a temple
of God and that the Spirit of God dwells in you?

1 Corinthians 3:16

*W*hen I first began teaching workshops on the topic of discerning God's voice, I would often begin by turning to the audience, which was filled with people sitting eagerly with pen and paper in hand, and ask them if they were absolutely sure they were in the right session and if this was really the subject they'd meant to sign up for.

That's because coming to this conference session carried some responsibilities that the other options they could've selected might not. I knew that what I was about to share would enable them to begin recognizing the internal promptings of God's Spirit. This would mean that they'd become accountable for obeying Him. That's the divine responsibility that accompanies the divine privilege we have.

So I'm offering you the same warning right now, because I'm fairly certain you'll walk away from this chapter with the capacity to begin hearing God. And that means you'd better be prepared to do what He tells you.

So, here goes . . .

Official Warning: If you're not prepared to begin responding in obedience to the voice of God, please don't read any further.

There it is.

Now, you still in? Even with that word of caution?

Okay, good. Let's go.

One of the clearest illustrations I've ever experienced about hearing God happened once when I was on an airplane, traveling from Dallas to Atlanta. I was lost in an enthralling book, enjoying an uneventful ride (which is always my preferred way of traveling by air), when suddenly our plane seemed to drop out of the sky.

A surge of panic and raw adrenaline rushed through the cabin. Some of the passengers screamed; some fell to the floor. Several overhead compartments burst open, sending bags and briefcases flying into the aisle. We all held on, imagining the worst and gripping the armrests for what seemed like an eternity.

Then, nearly as abruptly, the plane began stabilizing. Within seconds the pilot's voice came through the intercom, apologizing for the shock and explaining the reason for such a rapid, unannounced descent.

The control tower, he reported, had radioed the cockpit to warn of another aircraft located directly in our flight path. In order to avoid a collision, he had been told to lower his altitude immediately. From the pilot's vantage point, the other plane couldn't yet be seen, but the control tower had the whole picture in sight. If the pilot had acted only in conjunction with what his own limited perspective revealed rather than obeying the directive, our carrier and flight number would have been a "breaking news" crawl at the bottom of TV screens all across the country.

His readiness to hear from the air traffic controller and to trust the guidance he received had averted what could have easily become a major disaster.

The Holy Spirit is to us what the control tower is to an airplane pilot. The Spirit's ability to see what we cannot, and then communicate information to us based on His knowledge, provides us with insight we could never obtain through onboard instruments alone. And yes, sometimes what

He asks of us puts us in a place of discomfort that at the time seems unnecessary from our vantage point, but trusting Him and responding to Him is always in our best interest.

When we talk about "listening" for God to speak to us, as we did in the last chapter—discerning His voice, determining His will—the Holy Spirit is the One we're listening for.

And thankfully, by the grace of God, He is right here inside us. He is the primary means through which we will hear from God.

When you received Christ as Savior, the Spirit of God came to dwell within you, proof that you had entered into relationship with your heavenly Father. According to Scripture, you were "sealed in Him with the Holy Spirit of promise" the moment you believed (Ephesians 1:13). Therefore, "the anointing which you received from Him *abides* in you" (1 John 2:27). And this anointing, God's Spirit, was given to you in His entirety at the moment of your salvation. Not *some* of the Holy Spirit, not a first installment of the Holy Spirit, not a preliminary taste in anticipation of getting *more* of the Holy Spirit. "His divine power has granted to us *everything* pertaining to life and godliness" (2 Peter 1:3). God doesn't throw around a word like "everything" without totally meaning what He's saying. As a child of God you have all of the Spirit, all His power, all His wisdom, all His counsel, all His encouragement, all available to you, all the time. Whether or not you choose to allow Him to *fill* you by yielding to His leadership in your life is another story altogether. But this fact is imperative for you to always remember . . .

He's in you.

This means that listening to Him is an exercise in hearing from within—not being directed by external stimuli that divert your attention away from His direction.

Let's talk about how this works.

All human beings, saved or not, are composed of three parts: body, soul, and spirit.

- **Your body** is the material part of you—the part that ages and wears out over time—your hands and feet, skin and bones, the various organs that transfer blood and nerve signals and regulate all your physical systems.

- **Your soul** consists of your mind, will, and emotions; those elements that make you a unique individual with a distinct personality. Your ambitions, inner uniqueness, and emotional tendencies—each of these traits that others can readily recognize about you comes from your soul. Also enmeshed in this area of your makeup is your conscience. It is the moral regulator of the soul and is innate to every human being. It is what gives you a sense of right and wrong and communicates information that affects your thoughts, desires, and feelings about certain decisions, things to avoid, and activities to steer clear of.

- **Your spirit** is the true essence of who you are. More than just your visible identity or personality, your spirit is the part of you that longs for connection with a higher spiritual being. This hunger for God and greatness that's innate in every person—the human spirit—is what sets us apart from all other components of His creation. "We know that there is no real satisfaction, no real rest, except in Christ Himself. God made us with a God-shaped vacuum, and nothing will ever fill that vacuum except God," Elisabeth Elliot has said, and many others have expressed the sentiment.

Okay, still with me? Body, soul, and spirit. Everyone starts out with these. But before salvation, all three of these components languish in an unregenerate state. Stubborn. Resistant. Separated from God. Dead or dying. The minute we invite Him in, however, we are "in Christ" and have become "a new creature" (2 Corinthians 5:17). Our spirits are no longer separated from God but are reborn, recreated, regenerated. We can now connect with Him and hear His voice—something we could never hope to do before.

We've become utterly transformed, now and forever.

I never get over that!

But wait, it gets even better. At this point the Holy Sprit immediately begins the process of renewing us from the inside out. First our soul, and ultimately our body. We call this process *sanctification*. From His new position within our transformed spirit, the indwelling Holy Spirit starts to reform and reprogram everything about us until our attitudes, our emotions, our ambitions, and ultimately our whole personality and our actions begin looking and sounding like a redeemed saint of God. Which we are. To the glory of His great name.

So why the anatomy lesson here? Because understanding this incredible, inner change of events in your life changes everything about the way you hear His voice.

> Those who are in the flesh cannot please God.
> However, you are not in the flesh but in the Spirit,
> if indeed the Spirit of God dwells in you.
> Romans 8:8–9

In Good Conscience

My friend Rebecca was reared by a single mom who herself had been brought up by a single mom. In fact, as far back as she could see in her extended family, the cycle of divorcing for trivial reasons and then remarrying to counteract the loneliness was the norm. Experience and observation had taught her that this was acceptable behavior. She'd seen it up close in the people she loved, people who exercised authority and influence in her life.

So when Rebecca got married, and then came to those periods in her life when she and her husband weren't getting along—as all married couples experience on occasion—it didn't take much for her mind to begin contemplating an end to this relationship. She really had very few qualms with a "quickie divorce," if that was what she really wanted. Her conscience didn't kick up much of a fuss about that. No alarms went off. No serious danger signs.

See, that's the way it is with an unconverted conscience. Though it can be useful as a general guide, it's far from being airtight and infallible because our conscience is initially shaped only by things we absorb from the outside—like our own life experiences, personal environments, family traditions, firsthand exposures. So it's faulty at best. Though certainly helpful and accurate at points, our conscience has been seared by sin, shaped by varying sources and made susceptible to corruption by others.

It is *not* the voice of God.

But it *is* like a voice, right? I mean, those times when you've felt snagged by your conscience—maybe when thinking about taking home a spool of blank CDs from the office, or overestimating the value of your tax-deductible donations, or lying to someone about why you couldn't meet them for dinner on Thursday night—you heard something. It was your own inner voice, your conscience, and it did have a sound. You didn't hear an audible instruction in your physical ears, booming from the heavens, but there was no doubt you were being talked to. When "for some reason" you felt a sense of "rightness" or "wrongness" about hanging out with those people or taking on that opportunity, for example, there was just "something" in your gut compelling you one way or the other. That *something* is your conscience—steering you, directing you, and compelling you toward a particular decision.

Stop right now and think about it. Call to mind the last time your conscience steered you in a particular direction, or flashed up a warning sign before your eyes, or alerted you to a moral dilemma. Whether you followed its advice or not, you were still aware of an internal notice in your soul concerning something you were facing, confronting, or deciding on. You know how that feels. You know what it "sounds" like.

Remember it.

When the Holy Spirit takes up residence in you, He doesn't do away with your conscience. He awakens it. It's no longer just your own voice bubbling up from within. Like the rest of your soul, your conscience is being actively transformed by the Holy Spirit and becomes the mechanism He uses to relay the direction of God to you as it steers you toward decisions that reflect His perspectives. As you are diligent to allow God's Word and His Spirit to reprogram your conscience, it will begin to function with reliable data, thus responding differently—more accurately—regarding the decisions you are making in life. Much like a conference speaker who walks onstage and finds a microphone that's already on, the Spirit grabs our conscience and begins using it for His purposes. So the echo you sense within you is no longer just a composite of teachings from your own experience. It is progressively becoming a mechanism through which you hear the actual truth from the heart of God and the testimony of His Word. Trusted. Constant. Timeless.

This is why the *sense* you feel when God speaks to you is often a lot like that gut-level "knowing" you encountered when all you had to go on was an unredeemed conscience. The difference now, however, is that your conscience is being enlightened not only by your *own* views but by *God's* views on "sin and righteousness and judgment" (John 16:8) as the Spirit does His sanctifying work in you, and you cooperate by steeping yourself in the Scriptures and conforming your life to what He teaches you.

You now have a different Guide than mere good intentions.

Rebecca, for example, might hear certain members of her family telling her—informing the "voice" within her—to give up on this marriage. Life's too short. Why go around hurting like this? Get out and salvage what's left of your life with somebody who'll treat you the way you deserve to be treated. Originally, this kind of logic didn't stir conviction in her. But because she's now given her heart to the Lord and has begun renewing her mind with God's Word, Rebecca's conscience isn't the same one she brought with her into marriage. It's been changed, as *she* has. So instead of her conscience exclusively telling her to get out if she knows what's good for her, she senses a hesitation. Increasingly so, in fact, as she yields to His authority and lordship and hears the truth of God's Word convicting her through her conscience, assuring her of what she should do.

Assuring her from the inside.

As the apostle Paul said from personal experience, the Holy Spirit works in tandem with our conscience.

- **Romans 9:1**—In writing to the Romans about his anguish over the Jews' rejection of the gospel, he said, "My conscience testifies with me in the Holy Spirit."
- **Acts 23:1**—Standing at trial before the high priest and the Sanhedrin to defend his preaching, he declared, "Brethren, I have lived my life with a perfectly good conscience before God."
- **2 Timothy 1:3**—As he set out to encourage young Timothy in ministry, he described his own ministry as being done with a "clear conscience."

No matter how different Paul's opinions were from everyone else's, no matter how the masses despised his preaching, no matter how much persecution his ministry invited, he could still know he was doing the right thing because there was *agreement* between his conscience and the Holy Spirit. The Spirit confirmed within him—through his conscience—that the direction he was choosing was in conjunction with the will of God.

And it's the same with us. Over time, more and more, the farther along we travel in this often herky-jerky sanctification process, the voice we'll hear streaming through our conscience as we navigate the traps of life will more clearly reflect and confirm the directives of the Holy Spirit and will become an accurate steward of God's will for us. This will not be perfected, of course, until we see Him face-to-face, since we live in a fallen world that presents interference in our connection with God, but will continue in its transformation until that time.

He'll give you, for example, a red light of conviction, telling you to stop. Or a yellow light of caution, instructing you to hold back and wait a second. Or a green light of peace and permission, encouraging you to go ahead. When He does this, *celebrate!* It's living proof that the Holy Spirit is in there, working, guiding, changing your conscience from the inside out. Even if His direction seems momentarily uncomfortable, remember that He sees the whole picture. He's the control tower. He's protecting you from the disaster of your own uninformed inclinations. He's steering you safely into God's will, and He has your best interests in mind.

Many times I've made decisions against His prompting within me because I knew—*I knew!*—what was best for me. But every time I've done this, it's blown up in my face eventually. Whether it was wearing a particular outfit that made "something inside me" feel uncomfortable, or participating in an activity I "just knew" I shouldn't engage in, I've learned my lessons the hard way that God's wise direction is there for a reason. To help me glorify Him. To keep me from ending up again in the same old junk pile of regret and defeat.

He speaks to me deep down inside.

From His Spirit and confirming through the conscience.

I believe that God has related these somehow: the voice of conviction in the conscience and the Holy Spirit, the point of contact, witnessing within man's being. It is always perilous to resist the conscience within.

—A. W. Tozer

Copy That

So how do we really do this? How can we know that what we're sensing within is actually the voice of God? Since our conscience remains in the gradual process of change, with our hearts still bearing the taint of sin and our opinions still influenced by a worldly culture, how do we develop the ability to hear Him with a sure degree of confidence?

The work of God in bringing your spirit to life through salvation and then awakening your conscience through sanctification gives evidence that He *wants* you to know Him and to know what is the right thing to do. And because He's fully aware that you and I are not always very good listeners, His pattern is to say things more than once, in more than one way, so that if we're genuinely trying to listen and respond to His direction, we won't miss Him. This applies not only to the major decisions we need to make but also to the smaller details of life.

My experiences with listening for His voice (at which I still have a lot of growing to do) have led me to note the "five Ms" of correctly hearing God, helping us be more certain that we're accurately discerning the voice of our Spirit as He molds our conscience. Once you sense God might be leading you in a certain way, do these five things:

1. **Look for the MESSAGE of the Spirit.** Intentionally take time to listen and pay close attention. Turn your thoughts inwardly as you earnestly seek God. Consider what you are sensing in your "gut." Intentionally consider how your conscience is responding to the matter.

2. **Search the MODEL of Scripture for guidance.** You do this in three ways. First, stay immersed in God's Word so that your conscience will become progressively more sensitive to God's standards. Second, carefully consider if what you sense you're hearing contradicts the whole counsel or character of God as revealed in the Bible in any way. If it does, then the message cannot be from Him. Third, keep your eyes open when reading His Word for the moment when a Scripture just grips you, speaking directly and appropriately, even if surprisingly, to a particular circumstance in your life.

3. **Live in the MODE of prayer.** Take what you're hearing and direct it back to God. If an issue is troubling you or confusing you, don't waste time and energy worrying about it. Take it up with Him in prayer and wait patiently and expectantly for His answer.

4. **Submit to the MINISTRY of Eli.** First Samuel 3 chronicles the story of a young boy to whom God spoke. Three times Yahweh called out to him, and while Samuel heard someone speaking, he was unable to clearly discern who the voice belonged to. Only the mature and patient direction of Eli the priest helped Samuel realize that he was hearing from God. Seek the counsel of a mature believer. Talk to someone whose wise, biblical counsel you trust, and see if their advice mirrors what you've been hearing from the Word and from His inner witness.

5. **Expect the MERCY of confirmation.** Look for God's use of circumstances, Scripture, and other believers to confirm His direction for your life.

This last point is key. One of the best ways to discern the inner leading of the Holy Spirit is to watch how He continues to confirm His messages to you in ways only He could orchestrate, with shocking patterns of consistency.

I recall, for example, a time when I sensed God's Spirit convicting me to cut away some specific things from my life so that I could more sharply focus on my relationship with Him. Or at least it *seemed* as if that was the conviction I felt. Of course, it could have also been a legalistic trap I was falling into, or an overreaction to a passing thought, or a bit of hyperspirituality that would sure sound impressive if I were to share it in a group. Who knew? So I asked God for that final "M"—the "mercy of confirmation."

That very afternoon, my personal Bible study came from Deuteronomy 30:6, where Moses was teaching the Israelites to let God "circumcise your heart . . . to love the Lord your God with all your heart and with all your soul." Interesting. Later on, when I opened a book I was reading, the section scheduled for the day was entitled "A Circumcised Heart." Then at a Bible study I was attending later in the week, the subject drifted toward the theme of how God often allows shaking up to occur in our lives for the purpose of getting rid of some things that keep us from being fully His.

Hmm.

The Holy Spirit was going out of His way to communicate the same exact message to me, over and over again, causing it to ring increasingly true within my heart as His voice spoke from inside and confirmed it outside. I perked up to listen.

I'm telling you, God *wants* you to know His will. And He has chosen the Holy Spirit as the primary means to speak to His people—to speak where you can hear Him as you're faithful to confess your sin and to keep your conscience in constant agreement with Him—as you listen up by listening in. Listening deep. Listening early and often to the Spirit within you.

That's how you start to hear Him.

So it's too late, my friend, to turn back now. You've been warned. The next time you're shopping and see an item you really want, but something inside says "no"—it's probably God. The next time you're eating too much food and a sense of conviction tells you to stop—it's probably from God. The next time you're about to say something you shouldn't, and your conscience rises up to say you'd better not . . .

Don't.

You've just heard from God.

Obey Him.

Chapter Challenges

- Reacquaint yourself with the sense you feel when your conscience leads. Recall the last time it happened and record the feelings you experienced.

- Commit to the reprogramming process of your conscience by being diligent in the study of God's Word.

- Close this book and take time now to think about what your "gut" is telling you to do regarding a current decision you are facing.

- Ask the Lord to provide you with a godly, wise friend or mentor you can consult for counsel when discerning God's leading.

- Attune your spiritual senses to recognize His confirmations in your circumstances.

WHAT DO YOU WANT? *Chapter Three*

*God is working in you, giving you the desire
and the power to do what pleases him.*

Philippians 2:13 NLT

Jerry, my husband, is a city boy. The more modern, hi-tech, and refined his surroundings, the better.

And while I, too, enjoy the lights and sounds of city life, I grew up with quite a few country influences. My siblings and I went to camp as kids and participated in lots of outdoor activities like horseback riding and fishing. Jerry, on the other hand, was never exposed to any of that. Country living didn't hold any appeal for him. I got to see his first experience on horseback, and let me tell you, it was hilarious watching him flop around on that horse's back, his face a mask of disbelief.

Me, I find the sight of ducks on a pond or cows grazing in a field relaxing, but he only likes cows when they're cooked (medium well, thank you very much) and accompanied by a massive baked potato.

Before we had children, we lived in an apartment in the city, where we were exposed to all the sights and sounds you'd expect. We were two minutes from downtown and within walking distance from every restaurant and store you can imagine. It was a fun time. But when the children came, we knew we needed to be more responsible with our finances, so we put our dollars into a house. We moved into the suburbs and for nine years enjoyed our first house.

Two years ago, we decided to move again. And lo and behold, we found a perfect little house on a plot of land that made my heart sing. The two-lane road on which it sat was quiet and refreshing, and the trees, creeks, and wildlife made me smile. I knew this was *our* place and that our three rambunctious boys would have great memories growing up here.

Jerry, on the other hand, was hesitant at first. But after lots of prayer and godly advice from wise counsel, he sensed that God was leading us to purchase it. While he agreed the land was a jewel, living in this type of environment was not something he innately desired. Yet he decided to move forward in response to what he felt was *God's* desire for his family.

So we bought the house and moved in several months later. And Jerry prayed that he'd not just live in this new house but really begin to enjoy it.

It took time, but over the past two years my city boy has completely disappeared. It's not uncommon now to see him out on the property wearing a cowboy hat for shade as he takes pride in the lay of the land. In fact, his heart has been so turned to this little house, on this little piece of land, on this little two-lane road, that when the property behind us came up for sale, he considered it to be the best option for our offices for the Going Beyond ministry. So now, my former city boy lives and works on eighteen acres, owns a zero-turn-radius lawnmower, and carries a shotgun. And . . . he loves it. If he could, he'd spend as many hours of the day as he could out here. Just him and the cows.

He has been transformed.

What happens when you sense God's leading in your life, but you don't desire what He's asking you to do? Or you *do* desire something He's specifically asking you *not* to do? Or what if you're afraid to seek His will at all because you're worried He might require of you the worst possible thing you can think of? How do you deal with that?

Well, thankfully, when God speaks and leads you in the direction of His will, He doesn't just show up with instructions, a map, and a shove in that direction. Give Him the time He knows it will take, and He'll go a step further—He will literally change your desires to suit His purposes.

This is His spectacular work in the lives of His people.

When the new life of the Holy Spirit takes up residence within you and begins to grow His influence in your life, He changes your taste buds. Things that were once important to you begin to fade away, and you begin to desire new things. With a passion. Not because you've suddenly figured something out or forced yourself to be different, but because God has begun making His desires your own.

Listen carefully to the truth of Philippians 2:13 (NLT): "For God is working in you, giving you the desire and the power to do what pleases him." God's work in you is to cause you to desire His will for your life—to compel your mind, will, and emotions to be progressively transformed to align with His, then giving you the energy to carry out the plans He's mapped out for you to participate in.

We've actually seen this happen more than once in both our marriage and our personal lives. Time and time again, we continue to find that one of God's greatest miracles is what He does inside our hearts—turning our mind, will, and emotions until they line up with His plans for our lives.

Renewed minds begin thinking God's thoughts. Renewed wills begin desiring God's ambitions. Even renewed emotions begin feeling things they never expected to feel—not all at once but gradually, over time, as we allow His Spirit to alter our perspectives and motivations. He is constantly at work in us, sanctifying us, changing our personality to suit His design for us. And the more we surrender to Him and are conformed to the image of Christ, the less of a gap there will be between what He wants and what we want.

And we've been enlisted to participate in this process.

The book of James instructs us to "humbly accept the word God has planted in your hearts, for it has the power to *save your souls*" (James 1:21 NLT). This is one of the reasons why I went to such great lengths to describe our three-part makeup as spirit, soul, and body. Our *spirit*, you recall, was totally regenerated at salvation, but our *soul*, according to Scripture, is still in need of the ongoing touch of God's Spirit, still in need of His sanctifying, saving work.

And for this part, unlike salvation, He asks for our cooperation.

Immersing ourselves in the Word, actively listening for the Spirit's voice within, watching for His activity around us, and living in obedience to His directives—these are the ways we participate with the Lord's work in us. He promises to radically change us. And while this change takes place simply as a result of His presence within us, it is made most efficient when we do our part in conjunction with His work. This is one of the most incredibly supernatural aspects of our relationship with God: His Spirit truly makes us different. Because He lives within us—at the core of us— He can influence our soul to actually *desire* those things that are pleasing to Him, so that we're no longer rebelling against Him or serving Him out of duty but out of love.

With our mind, our will, our emotions.

With all of us.

And the more you participate in this effort, the more quickly and effectively you will see these results taking shape.

So whether or not you feel anything happening inside as you grapple with a decision He's leading you to make, I guarantee you a massive renovation is under way. More is happening beneath the surface than you can imagine. And as you continue to spend time with Him—listening, watching, and obeying—these underground changes will start working their way up through your soul and into the light of day.

So sit back. Wait. He is at work in you right now to transform the very core of you, even while you're combing through the contents of this page. And if it's truly His voice you're hearing, He will make you want what He says. Doesn't mean you'll love it right away or that you'll totally enjoy every aspect of it, but you'll discover a supernatural contentment with it, desiring intimacy with Him more than the prospect of disobedience.

Elizabeth is a living illustration of this. When I met her, she was a live-in housemother at a home for young women needing to get back on their feet. For various reasons, each woman had come to this house of hope and grace to recover from her past and get a fresh start in life.

As Elizabeth took me on a tour of the home, she explained the work they were setting out to accomplish, peppering her comments with sentiments expressing surprise at how she had found herself entrenched in this great work. She had always loved ministry but had found her niche serving children in Sunday school. This was her first love and had always been her primary ministry aim. And while she was willing to do whatever the Lord asked of her, she had secretly hoped that a women's ministry would never be on the list. For one reason or another, it just wasn't what she desired. But now, a decade later, her heart had turned toward these women and this ministry designed to help solidify their relationship with Christ and transform their practical experience. She never thought she'd enjoy this work. But over time, steadily and surely, it had become her heart's desire.

A favorite verse of Scripture says it best and most succinctly: "Delight yourself in the Lord; and He will give you the desires of your heart" (Psalm 37:4). This doesn't mean that He's necessarily giving you what *you* want, but rather that He is in the process of transforming your soul to desire what *He* wants. He is actually giving you His desires, and the more you delight yourself in Him, His Word, and His will, the more you can expect to see His desires implanted within you. We don't have to be afraid of what God's will might be. We can just relax in Him, knowing He will speak clearly, order our steps, and cause us to desire what brings Him pleasure.

It just happens. While you cooperate with Him in the process.

> I cannot control the voice of God or how it comes. I can only control my "ears"—my readiness to listen and quickness to respond.
>
> —Philip Yancey

What a Change

In Old Testament times, the Bible says that God led Israel "by the hand" (Hebrews 8:9), instructing them with external directions, delivered from the outside in. But as partakers of a new covenant, we are now being changed by His Spirit from the inside out. "This is the covenant that I will make with the house of Israel after those days, says the Lord: I will put My laws into their minds, and I will write them on their hearts" (v. 10).

His laws in our minds.

His word written on our hearts.

I'll never forget reading Psalm 46:10 during a time of personal devotion many years ago. I had read this verse numerous times before, but God was confronting me with it at a moment when I was extremely tired emotionally, expending energy on a particular pursuit that was wearing me down, leaving me drained and low on reserves.

His familiar words greeted me as though I'd never met them before: "Cease striving and know that I am God." A feeling of peace and serenity began washing over me, bathing my weary soul in His care and sufficiency. The Lord was removing my burden, asking me to sit back and watch Him work supernaturally in my situation. The Holy Spirit had allowed me to see something with my spiritual eyes that I had only seen before with my physical ones. All of a sudden, I understood the verse. It became relevant and personal to me, and it ushered me into a peace I'd not previously known in this situation.

He was writing His law on my mind.

He was speaking to me. Changing me.

And that's not the first time I've seen a change like this happen in my life.

Marrying Jerry was the best thing I ever did (or more precisely, the best thing God ever did for me). But when we first met, I must honestly say I wasn't all that interested. In fact, my first inclination was to try setting him up on a date with my sister! While I thought he was very attractive and I thoroughly enjoyed our friendship, my heart was involved elsewhere, which hampered me from being completely emotionally available for a deep relationship.

But as time went on and our relationship grew, I began to feel the Holy Spirit leading me to consider marriage with him. This leading was clear and had been confirmed in several different ways and by several godly people. So I prayed, "Lord, if this is Your desire for me, would You please cause my emotions to catch up?" I knew God wouldn't want me moving forward in marriage without a deeply rooted desire in my heart. So I watched and waited, being certain to remain open to God's will. And as I submitted myself to the authority of His Spirit within me, I *immediately* noticed a change in my feelings for Jerry. In a short span of time, they went from a warm, brewing casual sensation to a burning hot, passionately intimate emotion that took me by storm. God's purpose for me in marrying this man soon became my genuine, heartfelt passion. Jerry quickly became the apple of my eye and my true, cherished desire.

God was writing His will and His plans on my heart.

Making me want what He wanted.

He can do it, I promise you. I know from experience. If we surrender to the work He is already doing in us, we'll be surprised to find that where we once resisted His direction as being too difficult or risky or potentially embarrassing, we now find that we want it—at least more than we want the alternative of moving forward without Him. We'll find to our amazement that we don't even want what we used to want, that we're actually starting to desire and be drawn toward what we thought we never would.

And, wow, that feels good.

It's how a woman finds contentment when a dream has been deferred. It's how a person's heart becomes drawn to the mission field. It's how a man finds the desire to settle into his role as father when he never thought he'd want the obligation.

The Spirit does the work *for* you.

So try not to feel so burdened and overwhelmed, afraid of seeking and yielding to His will for you . . . whatever it may be. "For I am confident of this very thing, that He who began a good work in you will perfect it until the day of Christ Jesus" (Philippians 1:6). And part of that work is in your own soul—shaping it, conforming it, and preparing it for His plans.

There's a lot of freedom in that.

He writes His laws on our hearts and on our minds, and we love them, and are drawn, by our affections and judgment, not driven, to our obedience.

—Hannah Whitall Smith

Body of Work

The Spirit is not only able to transform our *souls,* making us want to follow His leading with our personal will, He also enables us to see a change in our bodies as well. In fact, that's His goal—to give us the power we do not possess in our own resources so we can experience victorious living— bodies that are subject to God's leading.

Have you ever sat in front of a second helping of some incredibly delicious, delectable indulgence and felt like you just couldn't help . . . but help yourself? I'll bet you can easily imagine yourself in this scene. You've already put away more food than you probably should have, and your mind and stomach are both sending you clear signals to confirm that. You're completely full with nowhere left to put another morsel, and you know it.

But your mouth has other ideas. It still desires what your stomach is telling you that you don't need.

Trust me, I know what I'm talking about.

This is a clear example of the disparity between what the flesh wants and the Spirit wants. "These are in opposition to one another," the Bible says (Galatians 5:17), warring to see which one you'll declare the winner today. So while your Spirit within is telling you to go one way, your flesh is watering at the sight of indulging itself with a turn in the opposite direction.

How do you win a battle like this—one you've fought and lost so many times before—forgoing what your body may want, choosing what the Lord wants for you instead?

Paul has the solution. You get in the habit of daily presenting your body as "a living and holy sacrifice, acceptable to God" (Romans 12:1), so that even your favorite indulgence doesn't have the last word. If placed before you at a moment when you just know that taking a bite would be contrary to what you're hearing from the inner voice of God's Spirit, you choose your satisfaction in Him, not in second helpings.

You let Him win.

And the victory ends up being yours.

You sleep better, you feel better, because you know better.

And guess what? This doesn't have to be all that hard. Paul simply says to give your body to God—make this one basic, catchall decision—and then live in the "victory" that's already been won for you by the Lord Jesus Christ (1 Corinthians 15:57).

Now don't expect to do this perfectly. It happens gradually, and—as we both know—none of us will ever become totally adept at it. We're still dealing with a body in the *process* of being changed, still very much infested with sin and fleshly desires. Even as seasoned believers, we can have a noticeable gap between what *we* want and what the *Spirit* wants, causing static to jam the airwaves when we're straining to hear His voice, even from such close range as within our own spirit. Even Paul struggled, as he tells us in Romans 7:14–15 (NLT): "The trouble is with me, for I am all too human, a slave to sin. I don't really understand myself, for I *want* to do what is right, but I don't do it."

Give Him your hands to do His work, your feet to walk His path, your back and shoulders to perform His ministry.

But if we'll keep listening, keep paying attention, and keep responding in obedience, we'll notice a miracle starting to happen. Right in these bodies of ours. They will no longer be in charge, compelling us to sin against the Spirit's directives within.

This is not because of the work you've put in to make yourself so spiritually self-disciplined and bulletproof. *This is God's work,* responding supernaturally to your cooperation, changing your body's desires just as He changed your soul's—lessening its influence and dominance in your life.

In the meantime, give Him your hands to do His work, your feet to walk His path, your back and shoulders to perform His ministry, your sexual members to enjoy His purity, your ears to hear His voice. Where you once allowed your body to partake in all kinds of sinful, rebellious activity, now you "present yourselves to God as those alive from the dead, and your members as instruments of righteousness to God" (Romans 6:13).

And the more you do this—the more sensitive you become to the

Spirit's prompting, the more successes He enables you to accomplish over your willful, demanding flesh—then the easier this all becomes, the more complete the miracle, the more direct the communication between your inside and your outside.

> The better you hear His voice and want to follow.
> If I have presented my body to Him as a living sacrifice, and I'm being transformed by the renewing of my mind, then I'm able to prove—to put to the test—what His will is. He will show me that which is good, acceptable, and perfect for me.
>
> —Kay Arthur

Immersed in the Word

I want to make sure you understand the importance of being immersed in His Word. There is not only a crucial connection between the transformation we've been discussing and your relationship with the Bible, but hearing a personal and specific word from God hinges on your commitment to His written one. That's where we begin to hear Him.

If you're serious about discerning the voice of God, then get serious about meditating on the Scriptures. Don't let your quiet time with Him—those times of purposeful Bible reading, prayer, and meditation—become a cliché of all duty and no devotion; these moments with Him are more serious than we think. The more you immerse yourself in the Word, the more closely your thoughts, emotions, and decisions will align with what the Spirit is saying to you and the more your flesh will lose its power and strength.

The Word's work in you is like having radiation therapy on cancerous cells that have invaded a person's body. You can't see the change happening, but the work that's taking place out of view is critical and worth every single treatment. When you soak in God's Word, the rays of His light invade your body and soul, burning away those things that are not like Him. Time spent in the Scriptures is vital. You might not see its work initially, but soon you'll have a bill of health that will prove it's been time well spent.

All day every day, from every conceivable source, your mind and heart are being saturated with messages that contradict God's truth—ideas that have a knack for working their way inside, scrambling the signals you receive from within, confusing the clarity of the Spirit's voice. They also encourage your flesh's resistance to God's will. If you do not consciously combat these cultural deceptions by saturating your mind in Scripture, your body and soul will be inclined to fall back to their natural, default positions, conforming to the world's standards rather than God's. By "fixing our eyes on Jesus" (Hebrews 12:2), we cooperate with the Spirit's work and make this sanctification process a whole lot smoother.

Listen, I know how tough this can be—prioritizing time in God's Word. I talk to a lot of women who come to me in tears sometimes, terribly discouraged because the demands of their current season of life make time with God's Word seem almost impossible for them. I totally understand. With three young boys at home, plus the multi-demands of ministry and other things, the day starts early around here and doesn't lend itself to many gaps in between. Time constraints and random interruptions are more the rule than the exception. There's homework to help with, stories to read, shoes to find, loud and lengthy bedtime requests to hear (and deny), and if you can spot a spare hour or so in there for some purposeful Bible study, I'd like you to come over to the house and find it for me.

If that's where you are, too—for whatever reason—let me toss out one solution that's worked for me and might at least accommodate some of the busier stretches of your life. This doesn't negate your need to make quiet time happen, but it's helpful for those days when, you know . . . it's just not happening.

Select one verse for the week, and write it on several index cards. Put one card on your bathroom mirror and the rest in other places where you're likely to see it frequently. Each day for seven days, recite and meditate on this verse while you wash your face, run your errands, wait in lines, and sit at traffic lights. Then even when you're at the playground with your kids, or sitting at your desk, or peeling potatoes for dinner, or preparing for a committee meeting, you can give this one single slice of His Word a chance to reverberate in your conscious thoughts.

Ask God throughout the day to clearly show you how this verse applies to the situations you're facing. Keep a record of the times He uses it to give you direction in your daily life. By the end of the week, this one verse will be so deeply etched and inscribed on your heart, you'll be able to carry it around inside you forever. You'll see how God uses His living Word to speak to you on a profoundly personal level and assist in transforming your soul to suit His plans.

This is what I fully expect to happen now as I continually present my body a living sacrifice, and as I immerse myself daily, regularly in His Word and in His way—and it's what He'll do for you.

I am certain He will give us the desire (if it's not there already) to do what He wants, conforming our wills to match His own. Knowing He's there working takes the pressure off.

Chapter Challenges

- Don't be hesitant or fearful to discover God's will for you.
- Cooperate with the Spirit's transformative work in your life by immersing yourself in Scripture, staying sensitive to His leading, and being obedient to His directives.
- Offer your body as a living sacrifice to God.
- Stay committed to God's Word even when it feels like doing so is not making any major difference.
- Considering the flow of your daily lifestyle, think of creative ways to keep the Scriptures front and center in your heart and mind.

WHAT'S BETTER THAN A BURNING BUSH? *Chapter Four*

When He, the Spirit of truth, comes, He will guide
you into all the truth; for He will not speak on
His own initiative, but whatever He hears, He will speak;
and He will disclose to you what is to come.

John 16:13

All of this stuff about our conscience and an inner voice and being given a new batch of wants and desires is nice to think about, but it also sounds like a lot of hard work. Have you ever just wished God would show you His will in a tangible, sensational way, like He did so many times in Scripture, something you could see or hear with your normal, physical senses?

Of course you have.

So have I. Whenever I read about the miraculous ways God often chose to lead the Israelites, I can't help but envy them. I mean, how incredible would it be for something as conspicuous as a cloud of fire to appear suddenly over your head and begin moving in the precise direction you were supposed to follow? That'd take a lot of the guesswork out, wouldn't it? I tell you, I'd love it, and sometimes I long for it.

In fact, today would be a nice day for it, as I'm right in the throes of trying to determine whether God would have me take on a new project that's on the horizon.

Looking at both the Old and New Testaments, we see Him speaking to His people in so many incredible ways:

- a burning bush (Exodus 3:4) and burning hearts (Luke 24:32)
- His glory (Numbers 14:22) and His humiliation (Philippians 2:8)
- a fire (Deuteronomy 5:24) and a cloud (Matthew 17:5)
- His name (Joshua 9:9) and His creation (Romans 1:20)
- visible signs (Judges 6:40) and an invisible Spirit (Matthew 10:20)
- visions (Psalm 89:19) and dreams (Matthew 2:12)
- teachers (Ecclesiastes 1:1) and evangelists (Acts 8:35)
- angels (Daniel 8:15) and apostles (2 Peter 3:2)

And the list goes on. Often the Bible doesn't tell us exactly how He chose to speak, only that "the Lord spoke," and those who heard Him weren't in any doubt about who was talking or what He was saying. Whether He spoke to reveal His character or to give specific direction, His voice was clear. Unmistakable. From the very beginning of time, and no matter what the method He chose, He has spoken in ways that could be plainly understood, revealing His deep desire to make sure that communication between Himself and His children was possible.

And though His methods have changed through the centuries—for His own wise and sovereign reasons—His goal has not. He has always wanted His children to hear, recognize, and obey His voice. He wanted it then; He wants it now.

Let's trail back through a little biblical history to prove it.

God, after He spoke long ago to the fathers in the prophets
in manyportions and in many ways, in these last days has
spoken to us in His Son . . . the radiance of His glory
and the exact representation of His nature.
Hebrews 1:1-3

History Speaks

One of the ways God spoke to His people as a whole in Old Testament times was through the person of a *prophet*. And the main way people could confirm the prophet's message was through a visible *sign*. Prophecy and signs went hand in hand.

For example, when God wanted to warn His people about worshiping false gods in the prophet Elijah's day, He instructed His servant to speak to them at Mount Carmel (1 Kings 18). Wouldn't you love to have been there for this divine display of God's authority?

First, Elijah challenged them to make up their minds who they were going to serve—God or Baal. And when the people wouldn't say, he proposed a little contest. The prophets of Baal would select two bulls. They would place one of the bulls on their own altar and call out to their god. Elijah would lay the other bull on God's altar and call on the name of the Lord. Whichever one answered by setting the wood of the altar on fire would be revealed as the one true God. Fair enough?

Well, this is when things got really fascinating, because despite their frantic efforts to get Baal to respond to them, nothing happened. Elijah even upped the ante by instructing that water be poured over the bull on the altar of the Lord. All that commotion, and then . . . nothing. But when Elijah walked up to the altar of the Lord and prayed, the fire of God immediately flashed from heaven and licked up the offering. "When all the people saw it, they fell on their faces; and they said, 'The Lord, He is God; the Lord, He is God'" (1 Kings 18:39).

First the prophet's message, then the visible sign to confirm it.

This happened numerous times, in numerous ways, all throughout the Old Testament (for example, Exodus 16:4–36; 1 Kings 17:1–7). Things changed, however, when Christ came. The Son was the Father's message to all mankind—a complete revelation of who He is and what His purposes are. No longer were prophets one of the primary ways God spoke to His people. When Jesus came and walked the earth, God began speaking through the person of His Son. And He, in turn, confirmed God's Word through miracles. *Christ* and *miracles* worked hand in hand.

We see this, for instance, in His raising of Lazarus from the dead. The message He was delivering to His people at that moment was this: "I am the resurrection and the life. Anyone who believes in me will live, even after dying. Everyone who lives and believes in me will never ever die" (John 11:25–26 NLT). So to confirm the truth of this message, He performed a miracle—calling His friend Lazarus back to life four days after the man's death.

What reason did people have for believing He was telling the truth when He spoke of being the "resurrection and the life"? Well, how about putting a dead man back on his feet again? Jesus backed up His Word with miracles.

But as He approached the time of His death, things would change yet again. He told His disciples that He was about to leave the world and would be going to His Father. "But I tell you the truth," He said to them, "it is to your advantage that I go away; for if I do not go away, the Helper will not come to you; but if I go, I will send Him to you" (John 16:7).

And how.

When the Holy Spirit arrived in Jerusalem on the day of Pentecost with loud noise, rushing wind, and tongues of fire, there was no denying that God was the source of these new developments. And by enabling believers to actually receive this Spirit inside themselves, God initiated the most personal way He still speaks to us today—directly through the Holy Spirit, hand in hand with Scripture.

See, in Old Testament times, not everyone who believed in Yahweh had the Holy Spirit also. He only came to specific people, at a specific time, in order to achieve a specific task. Whenever that task was accomplished (or sooner, if the person sinned and rebelled), the mantle and empowerment of the Holy Spirit was withdrawn (Judges 16:20; 1 Samuel 18:12). But after Jesus ascended to the Father, the Spirit became a permanent fixture in the lives of all believers. And ever since, He has attempted to reveal the mind of God individually and continually to every saint willing to listen.

Hold on, then. If things changed at Pentecost with the giving of the Holy Spirit, why is the remainder of the book of Acts—the chronicle of the first-century church—still replete with miraculous activity? Why was God still making His presence known in sensational ways (in ways appealing to the five physical senses) even after the Spirit had come?

The apostles and their close associates performed miracles in the early years of the church for the same reason Jesus had performed them—to confirm His spoken words, which had not yet been fully recorded. But once His Word was written down, there was no longer a need to *rely* on miracles as the sole validation of what He said. This doesn't mean that God can't or doesn't still perform miracles. It just means we don't have to *depend* on them to know when God is speaking.

We have His Word.

We have His Spirit.

The *Bible* and the *Holy Spirit* go hand in hand.

While each stage of God's chosen means of communication was different, His primary purpose has always clearly been the same—to allow believers the chance to hear His voice. So He carefully considered the best means for this to happen in the Old Testament, then during Christ's earthly ministry, and now after Christ's return to heaven. Like believers of old, we are still beneficiaries of a carefully considered, divinely selected option that the Father has chosen for those He loves.

> When God speaks, He does not give new revelation about Himself that contradicts what He has already revealed in Scripture. Rather, God speaks to give application of His Word to specific circumstances in your life. When God speaks to you . . . He is applying to your life what He has already said in His Word.
>
> —Henry and Richard Blackaby

Primarily Powerful

Does that disappoint you? This modern method of stillness and sanctification, of quiet listening for the Spirit's voice within you and finding confirmation through His Word—do you think it's somehow second-rate, second best? Would that burning bush still do it for you, as opposed to all this prayer and study and patience and subtlety?

Believe me, I know the feeling. It's so tempting just to want His voice to be big and bold, erupting on us all at once at high noon. Getting answers to our big questions about which school to put our children in, which church to join, which job to apply for, which doctor to choose—illuminated by a blowout sign from heaven that leaves no doubt which direction we should go . . .

What could top that?

But consider this. While we often wish we had what the people of God enjoyed in Old Testament days, I think they probably would have preferred what we have today—the special blessing of the Holy Spirit. They had no choice but to rely on prophets and visible signs since they did not experience the Holy Spirit as fully as we do in this age of the church. We possess a blessing they could only hope for—direct, personal contact with the living God. Even though His voice may sometimes be hard to discern without careful, deliberate discipline and self-denial, it's a gift that ages past would have envied. That's why we find the psalmist pleading, "Don't take your Holy Spirit from me" (Psalm 51:11 NLT).

So instead of wishing that God would "do something" to reveal His will to us, we should celebrate the fact that He has already *done* something, something mind-blowingly dazzling, by giving us the most precious gift of all and by providing an avenue to make His voice heard and known. Every time we kneel in prayer or read His Word and receive even a faint whisper of His wisdom, counsel, or conviction through His Spirit within us, we're enjoying a privilege our Old Testament brothers and sisters would have enjoyed immensely in their day-to-day relationship with the Lord.

The most spectacular way God has ever spoken to His people is the way He speaks to us right now—through the indwelling, intimate, incredible gift of His Spirit and the timeless, living, holy Word of God. And if we insist on seeking to hear Him *only* or even *primarily* in sensational ways—the open parking spot, the flip of a coin, the blindfolded pointing at a single Bible verse—we will miss out on the most personal means of communication possible with Him.

Be encouraged by this, my friend.

It's better than a burning bush.

But wait. Lest you think I've glossed over and quit believing that God can speak in obvious and tangible ways, I want to tell you something. While His primary means of communicating with us may be the gloriously gentle voice of His internal Holy Spirit and His Word—and while I'll freely admit that my normal experience with Him is not awash in Red Seas, Jordan Rivers, and talking donkeys—I'm not saying for one minute that God doesn't still specialize in miracles. He performs them all the time. I wish I could sit with you in a couple of rocking chairs on the front porch of some little bed-and- breakfast somewhere and spend the whole morning reading you entries from my journal. Then you'd know I wasn't playing.

God still intervenes in our world to make sick bodies well. To heal fractured emotions. To remove addictive desires from people's lips. To put $150 in the pocket of someone whose specific need is not $100, not $200, but exactly $150. Ask around, and you'll find somebody who's seen this sort of stuff happen up-close and firsthand. I know *I've* seen it. Miracles. God's handiwork. As believers in Christ, we can pray for and expect them from our heavenly Father, in accordance with His superior wisdom and timing.

So when I say we shouldn't *rely* on the marvelous and miraculous in order to receive information from His throne, I'm not saying we should stop anticipating it. He has not quit being astonishing. Our relationship with Him will still very often deal in the supernatural. That's what life in the Spirit is all about. He is neither unable nor unwilling to cause this combination of the Spirit and the Word to astonish now and then.

Leave room for God to be God.

Who are we to say what He cannot or will not do? I know some very godly, biblically grounded people who have heard from Him in ways that a lot of us would consider highly unorthodox. Yet I don't discount the sincerity of their encounter with God just because it's something I haven't experienced or would never expect of Him myself. I know God won't operate in a manner that contradicts His Word or proves Him to be acting inconsistently with the truth of His character. But just because we have a Bible and know our way around it pretty well doesn't mean we know everything about Him, or that some of our preconceived notions aren't little more than vain attempts to limit the Almighty.

I'd expect He wouldn't mind shaking those up a little sometimes.

Several years ago, in fact, God very clearly spoke to me in a way that I'd never experienced before. It was new, it was a bit uncomfortable, but it was so obviously God that I'd have been a fool to mistake it for anything (or anyone) else. It all started when I began sensing that the Lord wanted me to take a new direction spiritually and personally. I felt as if I'd become somewhat ingrown and partially blinded by the safety and familiarity of my Christian experience up to that point. My spiritual foundations had been sound and those who had helped me establish them were sincere and faithful saints. But there are times for stretching ourselves, for seeing what God will do beyond what we expect. And I'd begun to sense this burning in my heart, compelling me to expand my territory and increase my capacity, preparing me to experience God in a novel and fresh way.

I was hesitant about this. My personality is often a bit averse to change. I was a little fearful about what this would mean, not only for myself, but also for the ministry the Lord had entrusted to me. It would have been a lot easier just to bed down and make camp where I was already spiritually settled and established. But based on what I was hearing from Him in my personal prayer and Bible study, I knew the Holy Spirit was urging me to go exploring.

For some reason.

As part of my beginning stages of obedience in this area, I attended a brand-new Bible study. I didn't know anyone in the group and no one knew me—which is exactly how I wanted it, just in case things got weird and I needed to sneak out the back door. But at the end of the teacher's message that first night, he looked over in my direction and said something extraordinary.

It was a good thing I had come.

Now before I fully relate the rest of this story, I want to clarify something. I believe that the "word of knowledge" and "prophecy" (1 Corinthians 12:8, 10) are very real gifts of the Spirit that New Testament believers can be given as He chooses to distribute them. Yes, I fully understand the differences of opinion on this, but I see no reason for these gifts to be singled out for exclusion from the biblical text and listings.

There, I said it.

And even though I do not believe that prophetic messages that either add or take away from the Scriptures can be received as messages from God, I do believe that the Spirit gives to some people, on certain occasions, the divine ability to receive insight into another person's life. And when this happens, that believer has the opportunity (and responsibility, frankly) to share this scriptural message that applies to the other person's situation and affirms God's voice and direction.

You don't have to agree with me . . . as long as you keep on reading.

The Bible study leader said to me that evening, "I'm sorry, I don't know your name, but I just feel prompted to share something with you. I began to pray for you when you first came in, and the Lord gave me a mental picture of an old, rickety train track. It was ancient, but it was sturdy. Then all of a sudden, a futuristic, streamlined train filled to the brim with passengers came roaring down the tracks. I'd never seen a train like this one before. It was new and unique but was squarely fitted on that old, firm track.

"Young lady, I believe the Lord wants to do something new in your life, and it's going to be hard for you to imagine because it will be something you've never seen or experienced before. But there's no need to be afraid, because the old, strong, solid foundation of His Word will be what this upcoming work will find its footing on. And by the way, this is not just about you. There are a lot of people who will be coming along for the ride with you."

The tears were coming now. A kind stranger next to me handed me a tissue while the Bible teacher continued.

"'Forget about what's happened,'" he said, quoting from Isaiah 43:18–19 (THE MESSAGE). "'Don't keep going over old history. Be alert; be present. I'm about to do something brand-new. It's bursting out! Don't you see it? There it is!'"

Well, well.

Needless to say, this message shook me to the core. To be honest, I didn't know what to do with it other than believe it was God Himself. Hearing Him like this was unconventional for me. But I couldn't deny the relevance of what the teacher had said. Based on the inner witness of the Holy Spirit, I knew God was speaking to me.

So I just embraced it and kept my eyes open for the "brand-new" experiences He would bring my direction for His glory and the further advancement of His kingdom—not merely because I'd heard Him in a spectacular way, differently from my typical method of hearing the Spirit's voice, but because it totally confirmed what He had already been telling me. (Remember us talking about the "mercy of confirmation" in the "five Ms" from chapter 2?)

And, wow, has this message proven true in the years since. God has expanded our opportunities to serve the body of Christ in ways unique to our previous experiences. Through a series of events, we became connected with ministries to orphans in Uganda, anti–sex-trafficking efforts to rescue enslaved young women in Greece, and women's shelters in North America. Our ministry has been refocused from merely teaching from a speaker's platform to actually prioritizing outreach efforts that assist in the practical transformation of people's lives. The journey has been beyond belief. And far beyond myself. For His glory.

The lesson to learn from this, I believe, is twofold. God is definitely able to amaze us with His miraculous answers to prayer, or the occasional electrifying clarity of His message. This is part of how He speaks to us, and we ought to have our spiritual ears open to it. But we must not *depend* on these as if that's the only way we'll receive a word from Him. Such bombshells and surprises do not lay the *foundation* for us to hear Him. Rather, He may choose to give them at special times to provide *confirmation* of the messages we've already been receiving from the pages of Scripture and the Spirit's counsel. He has not promised to lead us in a way that appeals to one of our five senses but rather to our spirits—by the leading of the Holy Spirit within us. "For all who are being led by the Spirit of God are children of God" (Romans 8:14 NLT).

As His Spirit speaks, personalizing His message in a vast variety of ways, we hear His voice. Inside us. Compelling. Encouraging. Convicting. Challenging. Teaching. And guiding us right smack-dab into His will for our lives.

Chapter Challenges

- Make sure the following biblical template is in your knowledge base: (I) One of the primary ways God spoke in the Old Testament was through the prophets and visible signs. (2) The primary way God spoke during Jesus' earthly ministry was through His Son and miracles. (3) The primary way God speaks today is through His Word and His Spirit.

- Consider the primary way you've been depending on to hear God, and recommit yourself to the chief means He has chosen for this age.

- External activity should primarily serve as confirmation, not the foundation of hearing God. Evaluate whether you've been too quickly reacting and making big decisions based on outside observations alone.

- Remain open and willing to experience God in ways that are different from what you are accustomed to, as long as they do not contradict His Word.

- Commit yourself to praying for a complete openness to God's Spirit.

Part Two

RECOGNIZE THE SOUND OF HIS VOICE

HE IS
PERSISTENT *Chapter Five*

Once God has spoken; twice I have heard this.

Psalm 62:11-12

Knock, knock.

And who was there but my neighbor, right in the middle of the day, standing on the front porch wanting something.

I wasn't in the mood for company. Wasn't dressed for visitors. You've been there, haven't you? Then maybe you won't judge me too harshly for what I did—doing my very best to stay completely still and silent, as if I wasn't home, tucked away in my room until the knocking finally died down.

Give her a few minutes, I thought, and she'll surely get the message.

But she didn't. The more I ignored her, the more she knocked. Soon she was banging on the door as hard as she could, even calling out my name in a loud voice. So from the safety of my bedroom retreat, I emerged—before she came around and started peering in the windows, perhaps? I figured my cover was blown. I grudgingly scuffed down the hallway and answered the door.

And, boy, was I glad I did!

She hadn't come over just to chat. No, smoke was rising from the side of our house. Another one of my cooking experiments gone bad. A bit of grease left on the bottom of the oven had ignited, and before I knew it, flames were peering out from behind the range. It wasn't too serious, but tucked away in my bedroom, I might never have realized it if not for her persistent attempts to speak to me.

When God has a message for you, He is persistent. Like my unrelenting neighbor, He doesn't come to you just once and then go away figuring, "Oh, well, I guess she's busy now." No, when God speaks, you can expect Him to keep showing up, refusing to go away. Like with the boy Samuel in the temple (1 Samuel 3), the two travelers on the road to Emmaus (Luke 24), the woman Jesus met at a Samaritan well (John 4), or the prophet Jonah running away from the Lord's initial instruction, God keeps communicating until people recognize who He is and what He's saying.

So as you seek to hear the Spirit's voice in the specific situation you're facing right now—moving, a relationship matter, taking that job, trying to determine the best way to deal with a wayward child—whatever it is, ask yourself:

- What persistent, internal stirrings have I sensed?
- And how is He corroborating this message in other external ways?

When God speaks to you by the Holy Spirit within and also confirms it by other means from without, then be on the lookout for His directions. If you notice a consistent message confirmed through the leading of the Holy Spirit, the Scripture, your circumstances, and other people . . . pay close attention. God is repeating Himself to make sure you get the message.

Frederick Meyer, in *The Secret of Guidance*, said, "God's impressions within and His Word without are always corroborated by His providence around, and we should quietly wait until these three focus into one point. . . . If you do not know what you ought to do, stand still until you do. And when the time comes for action, circumstances, like glowworms, will sparkle along your path. You will become so sure that you are right, when God's three witnesses concur, that you could not be surer though an angel beckoned you on."

The Holy Spirit is at work in your heart, in the hearts of others, and in the events of your own life to point you in His direction. All of these things—and more—represent His unrelenting attempts to speak to you and cause you to listen. And honestly, the more massive and vital the decision you need to "land," the more lights you should require (and the more He will be faithful to provide) before you touch down on a decision.

When discerning the voice of God, expect Him to be persistent.

> Behold, I stand at the door and knock; if anyone hears
> My voice and opens the door, I will come in to him
> and will dine with him, and he with Me.
> Revelation 3:20

Still Knocking

Revelation 3:20 is often taught and preached as an appeal to the lost, reflecting God's persistence in knocking at the door of the heart of those who are unsaved. And while it *can* apply in that way, this passage was actually addressed to the early church at Laodicea—people who already believed in Jesus as the Messiah.

This is a look at God's persistence with His own people.

And in this case, the people were "lukewarm" (verse 16). Though generally pleased to be part of the church, they also had enough money to keep themselves comfortable and enjoy the illusion of security, so they apparently treated their faith and belief in Christ as a nice addition to their wardrobe. They took Him in small doses, as needed.

We're not surprised, then, to hear God rebuke them for their half-hearted spirituality. But what's stunning (and encouraging) is that God was still pursuing them, still knocking on the door of their hearts, still desiring a more intimate relationship with them. And He wasn't bashful about standing there as long as it might take until they opened up and let Him in. In the original language, the word "knock" is in the present tense. This is significant. It is a grammatical voice describing an action that is currently in progress with no assessment of the action being completed. The picture painted of our God is of One who continually knocks and knocks as He eagerly longs for a response of those He loves.

This act in the final book of the Bible reflects God's heart for connection with His people throughout the entirety of Scripture. In reading the Word, we see God persistently calling out in an attempt to turn deafened ears and hardened hearts back toward Him. And still today, He steadily, continually pursues His saints, even when they—even when we—are running hard in the opposite direction. He loves us, so He keeps it up. Never tires out. Never backs down.

He is persistent.

The book of Job reveals some of the persistent ways God spoke to His people in the Old Testament, in ways both subtle and shocking. Hear these from Job 33 (NLT):

- "He speaks in dreams, in visions of the night" (v. 15).
- "He whispers in their ears and terrifies them with warnings" (v. 16).
- "He makes them turn from doing wrong; he keeps them from pride" (v. 17).
- "He protects them from the grave, from crossing over the river of death" (v. 18).
- "God disciplines people with pain on their sickbeds, with ceaseless aching in their bones" (v. 19).
- "They lose their appetite for even the most delicious food" (v. 20).
- "Their flesh wastes away, and their bones stick out" (v. 21).

Okay, not all of these are pretty. But they do all have the potential to be highly effective. To get people's attention. In each of these examples, the Lord shows He is able to arrange events in such a way that they make His people realize He is speaking to them. Relentlessly. Until they listen.

The point to be made here is that your God can be counted on to keep coming. He won't throw His hands up in the air, wondering why you just don't get it. Nor will He hide His plans from you when He's ready for you to know what they are. He will consistently bombard your thoughts and your heart with His message until you're convinced of its authenticity.

Even if it takes a while.

Which it does, with most of us. We are nothing if not capable of missing His signals, wouldn't you agree? We don't always have our antennas up. We aren't always in listening mode. But He is well acquainted with this fact about us. He knows we don't always get good reception, depending on where we're located or where our head is.

So while we keep growing, He keeps speaking. And keeps speaking. First this way, then that way. Again and again. Over and over.

And when what we are hearing is *this* tenacious and is also in sync with God's written Word, that's the kind of voice to be listening for.

> The Lord leads us through His Word, through feelings, and through circumstances, and mostly through all three together.
>
> —Corrie ten Boom

Looking for Patterns

Many people are quick just to chalk up seemingly coincidental things to chance. One of my favorite romance movies focuses on this very thing, where a series of fortuitous occurrences brings a man and woman together despite unbelievable odds. Everywhere they turn, events conspire to bring them face-to-face—with each other, with their destiny—until the movie ends (as all good romances should) with the two of them together in blissful love.

Awww . . .

But in real life we shouldn't interpret the events of our circumstances so thinly. We should see our life happenings much differently than an unbeliever would. While to some a recurring pattern is just a simple reflection of how the "stars have aligned," we know better. We know that circumstances are controlled by the One who thought up "stars" to begin with.

Never think that the circumstances in your life have nothing to do with God's will. They have *everything* to do with it! When you're seeking His guidance, you should always reflect on the events the Lord is allowing to occur in your life. *Persistent, internal inklings matched by external confirmation is often the way God directs believers into His will.*

Stop and read that sentence again. Slowly . . . I'll wait.

As Beth Moore once said in an e-mail, "I know God is speaking to me about a certain matter when it seems like everything I hear or read for a while points toward the same issue. Anytime God gets 'thematic' with me, my ears start perking up."

Well said.

I've already shared several personal illustrations with you. But I offer another one here because I believe these really are instructive—and definitely real-life, as I can plainly attest. This type of thing is not out of the norm when God has a specific word for you.

A few years ago, I received a book from a friend on the subject of prayer. Okay, you know how books usually go that you get from somebody else. You start it. It sits around. You pass by it on the way to fix dinner and wish you had more time to stop and read. Finally it ends up at the bottom of a box or regifted to a friend for her birthday. But from the moment I picked up this particular book, I found myself unusually drawn to the spiritual journey of the author, and to the whole idea of using purposeful periods of silent prayer to more clearly hear God's voice. At the time, I'd never even considered anything like that.

Absolutely loved it. Read it twice, actually. All the way through. My heart just burned within me at what was being said. As a result I could sense the Holy Spirit calling me to engage with Him in prayer in a brand-new way.

Not long after the first time I finished reading the book, my personal Bible study led me one day to Ecclesiastes 5, where the first couple of verses say, "As you enter the house of God, keep your ears open and your mouth shut . . . After all, God is in heaven, and you are here on earth. So let your words be few" (NLT). Where had that line of Scripture been hiding all this time? Seemed as though somebody had sneaked a new verse into the Bible. These emphatic words leapt off the page and gripped my heart, confirming the message of the book I'd been so riveted by, as well as the sense I'd been getting all along from the Spirit's leading.

Then several days later, I was sitting in a meeting—does anything exciting ever happen in a meeting?—when one of the women seated around the table mentioned an upcoming retreat that some women from our church were going on. When I asked her a little more about it, she told me it was a . . .

No way. Did she say a *silent prayer retreat*?

I was so shocked, I literally dropped the papers I was holding—no kidding! Other than my exposure to the book I had just read, I'd never even heard of such a thing before that moment—women gathering together to spend a day and a half (thirty-six solid hours) in total, silent anticipation of the voice of God.

Talk about a circumstance lining up and making perfect sense.

Talk about a God who's persistent in His communication.

So when we got a phone call in the office a few weeks later from the Fox television network, announcing that they were creating a TV program on various types of prayer and asking if I might be interested in taking part, what do you think my answer was? I knew *immediately* what God wanted me to do. No doubt about it. He had used the circumstances in my life to confirm the direction He'd already been leading me from within. His perseverance had set me up to hear Him. His persistence had paid off.

Coincidence? I don't think so.

Circumstances can be just as sacred as a worship service when the Holy Spirit is in them. If He's orchestrating the events in your life—and He is!—He can meet you and speak to you anywhere.

But I need to interject something here. Seems like most of the stories we hear—like the one I just told—of people recognizing the voice of God and being able to respond with confidence always center around good things. Opportunities. Unexpected inflows of blessing. Exciting new possibilities. *Good* circumstances.

I guess those do make for the best sermon material and sound the most impressive on television. We'd be a lot more eager to listen for God and be watchful of our circumstances if we knew they were always going to be this enjoyable to deal with and produce such thrilling, immediate results.

But the Scripture is full of people whose most life-changing encounters with the Lord occurred while they were in places they did *not* want to be:

- Moses leading sheep in the middle of the desert (Exodus 3:1)
- Daniel in the lions' den (Daniel 6:16)
- Jonah in the fish's belly (Jonah 2:1)
- Hagar in a dry wilderness (Genesis 21:17)
- Gideon while threshing wheat underneath an oak tree (Judges 6:11–12)
- Mary and Martha grieving the loss of their brother Lazarus (John 11:21–27)

Obviously, God speaks through *difficult* circumstances too.

Have you got some of those in your life? Are you in a troubled marriage? Your umpteenth year of singlehood? Working a job you hate, or perhaps working just to find any job at all? Dealing with the consequences of a bad decision or sinful indulgence? Grappling with a medical test that's aroused your doctor's suspicions? Figuring out how to pay your first-of-the-month bills *and* fix the clutch that just went out on your car? Coming to terms with the fact that your pregnant daughter who lives three states away has been put to bed at six months of her term, and she really needs her mama right now?

Don't think of this as bad luck. Don't consider yourself off God's radar, with no need to be watching and listening for Him until things improve. Don't waste even these stressful moments of your life by wishing you were anywhere else, doing any*thing* else but having to endure this mess right now.

There may be something He's been telling you in private that He wants you to put into practice right here, during these very circumstances. Or He may be about to use this dry or dreadful season in your life as the catalyst to reveal an important, relevant message to you. This is not the time to wish you were in love instead of alone, or in full-time ministry instead of corporate business, or married to a saved spouse instead of an unsaved one.

God hasn't quit being persistent just because He's speaking in a tone or by way of a circumstance you don't approve of. Sometimes, in fact, His voice is clearest when we're in situations we don't prefer. Sometimes a pressing or ongoing problem, or a crisis that hits us out of the blue, presents the most conducive environment for us to draw closer to Him than ever. Sometimes we won't listen any other way.

And He knows it.

There's no such thing as a coincidence with God.

Will you watch and listen . . . even now?

> We know that God causes all things to work together
> for good to those who love God, to those who are
> called according to His purpose.
> Romans 8:28

All Around You

One final word on this subject. I've mentioned frequently how important it is for us to be in the Word, immersing our spirit in God's trusted counsel, giving the Holy Spirit the clearest opportunity for His wise, sanctifying voice to get through to us.

But running a close second in priority as we seek to make ourselves most receptive to the voice of God is the necessity of being actively engaged in a church family. Some of the best ways for us to hear Him speaking through our circumstances happen quite naturally, almost without trying, in the ongoing rhythms of church life. The Father uses His church as a means through which to make you aware of His plans and your personal connection to them.

How many times have you been sitting in a worship service or Sunday school class where a need is mentioned or a ministry is promoted that has stirred your heart? Perhaps it's a simple announcement from the pulpit, or a prayer request you overhear that causes you to become aware of a need you feel compelled to respond to. Or maybe you notice a person sitting two aisles over who, for some reason, the Spirit has brought to your attention and is instructing you to go over and get acquainted with after the service.

Simple yet critical opportunities like these are often the Spirit's way of revealing needs within His body as well as the gifts with which He's equipped you to satisfy the need. I would even venture to say that without connection within the church, you can never fully reach your full stature and potential in Christ. Why? Because your gifts were given to you in order to edify the church. And without an opportunity to do so, you'll never be doing all you've been called to accomplish. Being plugged into His church gives you an opportunity to discover His purposes and His personal plans for you within them.

To be clear, every need you see doesn't mean you've been personally called to be the solution. Don't be codependent enough to think that every problem is necessarily yours to fix or get involved in. But if you're truly, actively, purposefully listening for God—if you're already tuned into Him through prayer and Bible study and routine moments of stillness—you won't have to guess when He's calling your name to take part in a ministry request. It will connect with what He's already been revealing to you by His Spirit within. You'll notice a pattern pointing you in the same direction.

Ongoing opportunities to hear His voice—His *persistent* voice—are everywhere at church. He'll match the needs of the body with the gifts He's given you with which to edify it. Then when He wants you to respond, He'll stir your heart so that you'll know when to step into His will for you.

Be listening for that.

But there's more to be watching for at church than simply the bulletin board. By being a part of the family there you will find yourself in relationship with people who can call out in you what you might not see in yourself.

This is how Joshua first came to be in a position of leadership within the ranks of God's people. Moses appointed him (Exodus 17:8–16) to lead the Israelites into battle against Amalek, even though the Bible makes no previous mention of Joshua's prowess as a military commander. He didn't volunteer for the job and probably wasn't even trained in military tactics. Moses, as a wise and insightful mentor among the people of God, apparently saw untapped potential in Joshua, just waiting for a chance to prove itself. Being part of the family of faith placed a budding leader in the right position to be commissioned, groomed, and challenged, then elevated into service by someone who recognized his giftings and capabilities.

Many people's stories of success begin much the way Joshua's did. Throngs of people who have found their callings, served successfully in ministry, or even achieved a level of success in their professional careers can point to another individual whom God used as the catalyst to turn them in the direction of their own destiny. Maybe they didn't see their own genius or recognize their own skills and unique abilities. But someone else, standing along the sidelines of their life, took notice, encouraged them, and gave them the opportunity.

Think back on your own life. As you consider where you are now and where you have come from, who has God used as a tool to steer you in the right direction? Even more important, how might God want to use you to do the same thing for someone else? Every Joshua needs a Moses . . . and quite possibly, you are just the person that someone close to you has been looking for.

Not only that, but having a spiritual family provides all of us with people we can turn to for godly advice when we're unsure about something or needing prayer and accountability. I've already referred back to the "five Ms" from earlier in the book, in particular the "mercy of confirmation," which certainly applies to what we're speaking about in this chapter. The "ministry of Eli"—the process of bouncing what you're hearing in prayer and Bible study off the wise, trusted ears of your brothers and sisters in Christ—is one of the great blessings of being in ongoing fellowship with a faith community. It affords you the opportunity to rally with other believers and get their take on what's happening in your life, just as you can do for them.

We're not infallible, of course. What you say to others, or what advice you get from one of your good church friends, may not always be 100 percent trustworthy. You can't just run with what somebody tells you in such a context. But if you've carefully selected a wise, godly mentor, and if what he or she shares with you lines up with Scripture and with what God has been telling you on the inside, there's a good possibility you're getting at the truth of the matter at hand.

You're having a persistence moment.

You're hearing from God.

Once again.

That's just how He works. Nonstop. He doesn't want you to miss Him.

So I encourage you to rest in that. To be watching, yes. To be diligent, yes. To be purposeful about being quiet with God and then looking for Him in the external circumstances of life. Yes.

But always remember that He's the One who's faithful at being persistent.

As long as you keep a tender heart that desires to do His will, He'll keep speaking until you hear Him.

I'll even say that probably the best, most encouraging statement I've ever received from people who obviously commune with God and have walked with Him faithfully for many, many years is this: "I don't always get it right." Turns out, there are no experts at hearing from Him. Each of us is still learning on the job. So give yourself a break. Don't be too hard on yourself. Even when you hear incorrectly, God knows your heart well, and He honors the person whose sincere desire is to know and do His will even in their imperfection. "If anyone's will is to do God's will, he will know whether the teaching is from God" (John 7:17 ESV).

Because He yearns for you to know His will, the fact that you still make mistakes or get your signals crossed from time to time won't cause Him to back down or quit speaking. God doesn't count you out after you've moved forward in an area you thought was His will only to discover later that it wasn't. By God's grace, each miscalculation is another opportunity He transforms into your greatest teacher for hearing Him in the future.

So if your sincere aspiration is to know and do His will, remember He knows this as well. Do not let any failures cause you to become discouraged. He won't stop working with you. He'll keep knitting His counsel and guidance together through His Word, through well-placed circumstances, through His church body, and through whatever other way He chooses to get His message across. And as you continue to grow, through your successes and failures, you'll be more equipped to hear Him clearly.

So what are you supposed to be listening for when you're listening for God?

A persistent voice.

Chapter Challenges

- Look for a theme or pattern in both your spirit and external circumstances when discerning God's leading.

- Ask God to help you make the connection between His promptings and your circumstances.

- Plug into a local church, and be intentional about determining how your giftings can suit the needs of the body.

- Pinpoint a godly mentor whose life reflects a rich relationship with God and can serve as a wise counselor for you.

HE COMMUNICATES
PERSONALLY *Chapter Six*

I will give you the treasures of darkness
and hidden wealth of secret places,
so that you may know that it is I, the Lord,
the God of Israel, who calls you by your name.

Isaiah 45:3

*W*ent to the movies a few nights ago with my cousin. She's my "movie partner"—always up for a late-night flick. Once her four little girls and my three boys have been fed and put to bed, we can make a break for the theater. Two hours of mindless entertainment.

Last week we sat through one that kept us laughing hysterically during many scenes, not the least of which was when a couple with eight children was trying to control their gregarious brood. The father, intense and direct, was working valiantly to corral a few that were running up and down a staircase in someone's home during a gathering. As he tried to call them to attention, he stammered through their names only to finally get so discombobulated, he stopped and asked his wife, "What's *that* one's name?"

Our *heavenly* Father, on the other hand, doesn't have this problem. He isn't frantically searching for your name in His memory bank. God knows exactly who you are, never loses track of you, and has a personal message with your name on it.

Just for you.

Many times in Scripture when God spoke to people, He used their given names and intersected their lives right where they were.

- When He wanted to speak to a confused little boy ministering in His temple, He called the child by name: "Samuel! Samuel!" (I Samuel 3:10).

- When He wanted to get the attention of a weeping woman seeking the body of her crucified Lord, He called her by name: "Mary!" (John 20:16).

- When He wanted to reroute a man traveling toward Damascus to persecute Christians, He called him by name: "Saul, Saul" (Acts 9:4).

He knew who and where they were, just as He knows those same details about you. He knows *you*. Personally.

He knows, for example, if you're a fledgling believer or a seasoned saint. He knows if you're hardheaded or more sensitive to His soft prodding. He doesn't discard you or fault you for your weaknesses in hearing Him. Like Samuel, like Mary, like Saul—God meets you where you are. He speaks in a way He knows you can hear Him.

You don't need a seminary degree for this. You don't need certification in spiritual discernment. Hey, you don't even need to finish this book (although I hope you will!) in order to hear God's personal word for you.

For some reason we've been duped into thinking that God only speaks to certain people and only in ways that these "elite" saints can understand. But even in biblical times, the opposite seemed to be true. Jesus didn't use a churchy vernacular that only a particular type of person could comprehend. As author Jan Johnson notes, "Jesus spoke in everyday Aramaic, and the New Testament was written in *koine* (or common, not classical) Greek; so today, God speaks to you in everyday language." Jesus used everyday language to communicate with regular, ordinary people, while the religiously astute and the social elite often stood on the sidelines.

Please don't feel like you're being left out while God communicates with His superstars and leaves you and me and the rest of us on our own to do the best we can. He doesn't count the hairs on your head for no reason.

He wasn't acquainted with you before you were born only to forget about you now. Rise up with confidence that your God and Father has something distinct and deliberate to share with *you*—right in your own living room, in your current set of circumstances—a special delivery from Someone who doesn't need to wait for your Christmas list to know what you truly need to receive from Him.

When God speaks, He addresses His message personally.

He's talking to *you*.

> When He speaks, it's in a language of our personal lives,
> through a verse or passage of Scripture that just seems to leap
> up off the page with our name on it.

—Anne Graham Lotz

Same Destination, Different Directions

Today, of course, God speaks to us through the Holy Spirit, embedded inside us. He is our personal tour guide through the journey of life, giving us private instructions designed specifically for us. He knows our current stage of spiritual development and can find us wherever we are in the journey of our lives. He is fully aware of the plans He has in mind for us, and can be trusted to direct us accordingly, instructing us in the way we should go.

The way *we* should go. Personally.

I'm not saying, of course, that His truth is relative. There's no such thing as *your* truth and *my* truth. But because His knowledge of you and His designs for you are extremely personal, He will apply His truth to you in a way that's as unique as your circumstances are.

> *Never* expect the Holy Spirit to speak anything to you that's contrary to what's written in Scripture.

And therefore, the outworking of His principles in your life and mine can possibly look extremely different.

Certainly the Bible contains many statements and principles that are black-and-white, things that apply at all times, in all places, to all people. We may try to skirt around these or convince ourselves we're justified in doing things differently in our particular case, but . . . no. We're not. If God's Word takes a stand on an issue that you're facing, there's really no need to waste your time praying and fasting about it or seeking a personal word from God on the issue. You've already gotten His answer on the subject, and you need to just run with it. Never expect the Holy Spirit to speak anything to you that's contrary to what's written in Scripture. You'll be waiting a long, disappointing time if you do.

However . . .

The Bible does not expressly address every question or situation you may be dealing with at the moment. When you need to decide whether to move or stay put, whether to accept that job offer or keep looking, if you should teach Sunday school for another term or if it's time to pass the baton, you need God's specific guidance that's customized to you and your situation.

And this is where His incredible Holy Spirit comes in. You can expect Him to lead you personally because He cares about even the most insignificant details in your life and is eager to tell you which direction you should take. He will give you a personal conviction about these matters as He uses the truth of God's living Word to speak specifically to your situation. When He does, you should be careful not to hold others to the standards God has set for *you*.

What might this look like? For the woman He's calling to be a full-time mom, the Spirit may give a personal conviction about not working outside the home. For the man directed to lead a Bible study, the Spirit may limit the amount of time he can spend watching TV or socializing so he can invest himself in preparation. For the woman being led to homeschool her children, the Spirit will instruct her not to pursue more traditional, mainstream educational options.

He may even direct you to place a *temporary* restriction on yourself, like steering clear of certain foods for a while, or certain shopping experiences, or certain entertainment options—all for a particular purpose He needs to perform in you, something He's especially preparing you for at this current season of life. Any kind of prompting like this from God's Spirit is specifically designed for you—the person to whom He's speaking—to foster *your* needs, to care for *your* family, to orient *your* life. And you should trust what He's telling you.

It's personal.

It's for you, individually.

My friend Karen, for example, is one of the godliest women I know. She has an intimate relationship with the Lord and listens intently for the Spirit's voice. She eagerly wants Him to steer her choices and is faithful to let Him do it. So because of her personal convictions, she follows a code of conduct that many would consider unnecessarily rigid.

Now while a woman's modesty is indeed a clear mandate from Scripture, this fleshes itself out in a very unique way in Karen's life. As she works in ministry to evangelize and disciple young women immersed in a certain cult dynamic—one that forbids them from wearing pants—she feels led by the Lord not to do so herself. For Karen, the principle of modesty requires that she avoid certain outfits in order that her outreach can be most effective. So even when she's just hanging out with us, her friends, she still abides by this personal conviction.

If we wear or buy something that, while not immodest, goes against what Karen's personal permission slip from the Holy Spirit allows her to do, she is pleasant, polite, and gracious. She's not prudish about it at all. Doesn't try to impose her convictions on us or get us to change our outfit preferences to suit her. Doesn't make us feel like we're awful for wearing certain popular fashions (although I'll admit, it does sometimes make us look at each other and ask, "Should we really be wearing this?"). Karen just smiles, compliments us on what we're wearing when she so desires, and humbly responds to God's personal leading in her life.

The point is, while we are not sinning to wear this attire, *Karen* would be—not because there's something wrong with the clothes themselves, but because God has given her personal counsel that something is wrong with certain kinds of clothes for *her*.

When He gives you a personal message—and He will!—don't hold others accountable to it, as though it's some global statement that applies to all believers, as if you've now become the legalistic guardian of everyone else's conscience. This is what God is saying to *you*. It's what He's requiring of *you*.

It's personal.

Like He is.

Do not let what is for you a good thing be spoken of as evil.
Romans 14:16

Personally Speaking

When I need to drive into downtown Dallas from out where we live, I take the main road, north on Highway 35. I think it's the most efficient and obvious way for anyone to go. *And it is*—for me. But some people who live in our area choose a different route into town from the one I'd pick. Mine, you see, is not the only way a person could be led to go and still end up in the same place. An alternate path or method might be best for somebody else.

As God leads us through our journey of life with Him, He marks out different avenues for each of us within the overarching guidelines of Scripture, drawing an individualized map for us to follow. Others may not choose our road—*and they shouldn't* if it's not the map they've been given. Each man and woman is responsible for following the Lord according to the way God has personally led them, bringing glory and honor to Him by their obedience to His instructions. Our job is not to judge others but to give our fellow believers the freedom to be who the Lord has led them to be, while being sure we're following God's individual leading in our own lives.

So when you receive a personal word from His Spirit, embrace it. Enjoy it. Consider it a space within which you are free to follow God and His unique plans for you to the absolute fullest. Even if some people take a different view—be it a matter of childhood discipline, or personal appearance, or technology use, or worship style—you don't need to feel bound by what God is customizing to others' lives. Their opinion or restriction is not yours, just as your opinion or restriction is not theirs. We are only accountable to the Lord, to the boundaries of Scripture, and to whatever He personally requires of us as He applies it to our lives by His Spirit.

I have a personal conviction, for example, about drinking alcohol, even though nowhere in the Bible does God tell us specifically not to drink. The only indisputable teaching on the subject—to which every believer must be held accountable—is not to get drunk. So even though I know many godly people who responsibly enjoy a glass of wine with dinner or at a social gathering where drinks are served, I myself always feel a twinge of conviction about consuming it, so . . . I just don't. The Lord has not given me the freedom to drink and be okay with it.

Therefore, other people's freedom in this area is not a cue for me to loosen my convictions, nor is my personal prohibition against drinking meant to limit what those around me feel permitted to do without guilt. When two alternatives fall like these within the general teaching of Scripture, the Lord can lead two believers (who equally love Him) in completely opposite directions. One yes, one no, yet each walking in line with God's personal word to that individual.

But—"remember, it is sin to know what you ought to do and then not do it" (James 4:17 NLT).

This is where it *really* gets personal.

When you recognize that the Holy Spirit has given you specific insight and direction on a matter, and you sense that your conscience is giving you assurance to confirm that leading, yet you deliberately go against it—even if it's something the Bible doesn't clearly come out and say—you weaken and desensitize your conscience, and you sin against God. Even if the issue is as seemingly trivial as eating more than you should, or taking a particular type of job, or wearing a certain outfit, or shopping at your favorite outlet store, if the Spirit is leading you to do (or not do) a certain thing, then yield to His personal word in your life. It's your Father's way of calling you by name, leading you toward His desired destination *for you*. He knows you so well, and loves you so completely, that He has mapped out a path that is distinctly yours. He has a purpose, a reason, for bringing you this way.

Take it personally.

You will make known to me the path of life; in Your presence
is fullness of joy; in your right hand there are pleasures forever.
Psalm 16:11

God Is Love

There's another important aspect of the personal nature of God's voice
that I want to take time to share with you. One of the ways that God is
most intimate and shows personal care for His children is by revealing His
great and abounding love. When a message or inner voice you are sensing
makes you feel condemned or burdened by a cloak of guilt, then it is probably not from God. If the foundation of the conviction you are feeling or
the direction you are sensing stems from fear or condemnation, then you
can be sure the Enemy is behind it.

I've seen this happen myself.

When I went off to college, I left the sheltered life of my Christian
family, school, and friends, and entered another world. But I was actually
pretty excited by the prospect of a new, independent lifestyle. Maybe a little
too excited. I soon found myself living in a way that I knew wasn't pleasing
to the Lord. As a result, even though graduation day brought an end to my
college years, it did not end some of the condemning thoughts I continued
to struggle with in the years that followed. No matter what I accomplished
or how far I removed myself from the poor choices of my past, a nagging
voice inside my head kept pouring on the guilt.

I had sought God's forgiveness as fervently as I knew how, but I couldn't
seem to completely erase the grief and regret. They were like dark, heavy
clouds hanging over my head, and they could show up at any time, tripping
me up, pushing me down.

That is, until the Spirit led me to this refreshing verse of Scripture: "I,
even I, am the one who wipes out your transgressions for My own sake, and
I will not remember your sins" (Isaiah 43:25).

"... *will not remember* ..."

With these loving words, the Lord made clear to me that His goal is never to bring guilt and condemnation by continually reminding us about the sins of the past. Rather, He wants to bring healing and restoration by forgiving our sin and throwing it into the sea of His forgetfulness. God's desire is to lovingly lead us into His grace.

He leads us forward, not backward. And realizing this truth can make a world of difference in our ability to accurately discern when God is speaking, as opposed to when we're being coerced by the Enemy, who craftily (and often very effectively) uses our guilt and shame as a tool to steer us incorrectly.

So if the message you're hearing as you seek to discern His personal will and plan for your life is condemning or rooted in fear and intimidation, making you feel unworthy or incapable, then it isn't the voice of God who

You'll know the Spirit is speaking to you personally about your sin when the feeling you get is not despair but a fresh desire for holiness and purity.

loves you. It is the voice of the Enemy, seeking to use your vulnerability to deceive you.

God's character and His purposes toward you are definitively captured in Scripture, and perhaps never more clearly so than in this simple way: "God is love" (1 John 4:8). Love is who He is and what He invites you to experience with Him. So when He speaks to you, He may *reveal* sin. He may bring it out into the open for you to confess and deal with. But His goal in doing so is to cleanse you and change you. He doesn't want you acting out of guilt or a fear of rejection, but rather out of a love relationship with Him.

He knows what you've done. He knows you personally and intimately enough to know everything about you, even what no one else knows, not even the people who know you the best. But because "God is love," He will not use His knowledge against you.

He loves you. Personally.

So it's worth the time spent to carefully consider the bottom line of what you're hearing. When you boil it down to its foundation, do you sense the warmth and love of God? Or do you instead hear the accusatory tone of the Enemy of your soul? Learning to recognize the difference between the Enemy's *condemning* voice and God's *convicting* voice is a great tool for determining God's leading in your life. To *condemn* means to consider something worthy of punishment. To *convict* means to bring something to light in order to correct it.

The Enemy's voice can cause you to feel guilt with no clear means of relief. Nothing but heaviness and hopelessness, often with no specific connection to a particular sin. Just . . . there. Take *that*! But when the Spirit brings conviction—which is many times the purpose of His personal message to you—He will also bring you a road map, a way back, a way out. He has no desire to pummel you and prevent you from getting up again. Far from wanting to harm you, He is initiating freedom and blessing in your life.

With Him, there is "no condemnation" (Romans 8:1). No ridicule. Total love. Love for you.

You'll know the Spirit is speaking to you personally about your sin when the feeling you get is not despair but a fresh desire for holiness and purity. You'll know it's God when He's calling you back to His side, not tossing you out like yesterday's garbage.

> The purpose of the voice of condemnation is to push you away from His presence—that which is the very source of your victory. The purpose of the voice of conviction is to press you into the face of Christ.
>
> —Bob Sorge

No Condemnation

John 8 tells the story of a group of scribes and Pharisees (a particular branch of Jewish legalists) who caught a woman in the very act of adultery. Dragging her forcibly into the temple area where Jesus was teaching, they hoped to publicly expose her sin and put Jesus on the spot.

How must this woman have felt? Imagine someone snagging you by the back of your neck at a weak, sinful moment and dragging you from there into a Bible study at church where some of your best friends were gathered.

These men had no desire to help this woman out of her sinful lifestyle or to seek restoration for a life being lost to misplaced desire. Their aim in using her was to expose, embarrass, and disgrace her, discrediting Jesus in the process.

This is Satan's goal as well, still today. Still with us. Can you hear him even now?

What's he been accusing you of lately?

But look at what a different story it was when Jesus got involved in the situation. With the crowd demanding that the law of Moses be upheld, and eager to see what Jesus was going to do, He said in everyone's presence, "He who is without sin among you, let him be the first to throw a stone at her" (verse 7).

Dead silence.

The accusers realized that they didn't qualify. None of them. One by one, they slinked away.

The only One who had the right to call her out and take her life was the One speaking—the One who knew even *this* woman personally. This vile woman . . . adulterous . . . guilty. But even knowing her like He did, He did not throw the stone.

Did you hear what I just said?

He did *not* throw the stone.

I ask you to bury this truth deep within your heart, so that you will more clearly recognize the voice of God speaking to you personally. He alone has the right to condemn you for what you've done—for *all* you've done—yet He has chosen instead to bestow grace on you despite everything. He didn't throw stones then, and He doesn't throw them now.

"Where are they?" He asked the woman that day. "Did no one condemn you?"

She said, "No one, Lord." And Jesus said, "I do not condemn you either. Go. From now on sin no more" (verses 10–11).

He didn't ignore the woman's sin. Didn't make excuses for it. He just didn't condemn her for it. God's voice will *convict* us—will point out our sin—but He will also express His love for us. He won't *condemn* us or burden us with guilt. Rather, He will offer us enough grace to leave our sin behind and continue on in righteousness.

So whenever I feel the pain of "stones" being thrown at me, I quickly realize they aren't coming from my loving heavenly Father. He convicts me, but He doesn't condemn me. How do I know this? Because I know where condemnation comes from. So do you.

So don't listen to it.

Jesus Christ bore the punishment for your sin once and for all on the cross. Therefore, when God speaks to you now, His words will not dispense judgment. They may reveal your shortcomings so you'll recognize your sins—especially those sins you didn't even realize you were committing. But He will buffer this revelation with His grace, His love, and (wonder of wonders) His second chances. While condemnation points out a problem only to judge you and make you feel guilty, God's soothing, personal words of conviction offer you a remedy, a hope, and a way forward.

> *The* character of God will come shining through when He speaks to you. If it doesn't, it's not His voice.

You'll know His voice by its loving, personal tone.

So when determining whether or not you're hearing from God, always consider His "Fatherliness." The Scripture paints a picture of One who loved you so much that He gave the life of His only Son to eliminate every inch of separation between you. His goal for you since the beginning of time has been to enjoy close, intimate, loving fellowship with Him. Personal relationship. That's the way He wants you to know Him.

That's the way He knows you.

The character of God will come shining through when He speaks to you. If it doesn't, it's not His voice. But when it does—whether convicting, or counseling, or calling you toward a certain conclusion in regard to a specific matter in your life—draw near to Him with a heart eager to do what He's telling you.

Like Samuel (see 1 Samuel 3), say to Him, "Speak, Lord, for Your servant is listening."

And expect Him to answer you.

Personally.

Chapter Challenges

- Keep yourself continually reminded that God knows where you are on your journey with Him, understands your weaknesses and proclivities, and can still speak to you personally.

- Be emphatic about your obedience to God's directions while being careful about holding others to your personal convictions.

- Don't allow other people's convictions to direct your decisions or cause you to feel guilty about the freedoms the Lord has given you.

- When discerning God's leading, consider whether what you are sensing is based on fear, guilt, or intimidation, or whether its foundation is the love, care, and concern of your loving Father.

HE BRINGS PEACE

Chapter Seven

These things I have spoken to you,
so that in Me you may have peace.

John 16:33

*I*t just didn't make sense. Moving from a middle-class neighborhood in a plush, suburban area to an urban community known for the things you'd normally try to avoid was utterly ridiculous.

But they did it anyway.

This young, successful couple had worked their way up within growing careers. When they started their family, they had clear aspirations for the type of lifestyle they wanted. And while they knew they couldn't plan every little detail of their bright future, no version of the story they'd written had included this.

But God had spoken. First to him, and then slowly, progressively to her. Over time, God's Spirit had made His call completely clear. They were to give up life as they'd known it and planned it, and begin ministering to people in the city. And they weren't to do it by day and then escape it by night. They were to live among those whom they were called to serve.

All kinds of red flags and objections were raised, but in spite of it all, they had one thing going for them—something that can make a man or woman of God persevere against any amount of difficulty and second-guessing.

They knew—by continued confirmations through His written Word and by corroborating circumstances surrounding their decisions—they knew they'd heard from the Lord.

And so, they had *peace*.

So despite the naysayers, this family moved forward in faith and obedience, expecting to see God's supernatural activity at work. And today, their ministry has had a profound impact on hundreds of families whose futures have been transformed because of one couple's choice to hear and to heed God's Word.

God's peace makes all the difference.

In the days and hours before Jesus went to the cross, He comforted His disciples by telling them that He would not be leaving them without guidance or direction after He was gone away. And He promised them His *peace*—a permanent, restful assurance no obstacle or opposition could diminish or destroy, a peace no enemy could touch because it would rest deep within their hearts, locked in their very souls.

"I am leaving you with a gift," He told them, "peace of mind and heart. And the peace I give is a gift the world cannot give. So don't be troubled or afraid" (John 14:27 NLT). At a time when His followers were surrounded by anger, frustration, and death, Jesus was assuring His disciples that with *real* peace—*His* peace—even the most dreadful of circumstances could not tamper with their serenity. "Here on earth you will have many trials and sorrows. But take heart, because I have overcome the world" (John 16:33 NLT).

Jesus was so focused on peace, in fact, that the first words He spoke to His followers, within hours after His resurrection, were these: "Peace be with you" (John 20:19). Showing them His pierced hands and feet, He repeated Himself: "Peace be with you" (verse 21). With these words of blessing and reassurance still lingering in their ears, the Scripture declares that Jesus then "breathed" on His disciples, bestowing on them the gift of peace Himself in the person of the Holy Spirit (verse 22). God's unshakable, internal solace would now be their constant companion.

They were to know Him by His peace.

And so are we.

So are you.

When God speaks, not only will He be *persistent*—speaking from within and confirming from without the word He's communicating to you; not only will He be *personal*, but He will also cause the cumulative effect of these characteristics to release into your soul a *peaceful assurance*—a peace you can sense deeply, even when chaos is swirling around you. Like an anchor holding a ship steady, God's peace gives security. It's a peace that doesn't flutter for a few seconds and then evaporate into thin air, but one that refuses to go away, hours later, days later, months later—even when the path ahead is blocked by all kinds of challenges, risk, and danger, and even if you'd rather not go in the direction it is pointing you. Your own

Peace is not only an element of His character; it's evidence of His presence.

heart, left to itself, might quiver and hesitate and ultimately fail, but the Spirit's peace soothes and strengthens you, giving you confidence to accomplish the task He's sending you out to perform.

You'll come across many things in life that you'll seem ill-equipped to handle—let's face it, you and I *will* be ill-equipped to handle them—perhaps a new opportunity, perhaps an unexpected trial. Yet you'll get the sense that God is leading you to do something specific in the midst of it. It scares you, maybe because you don't know how to do it. Maybe others think you're crazy even to consider the course of action God has led you to pursue. Maybe they feel sorry for you that you have to endure something so difficult. But as a sure sign of His grace, love, and mercy, God gives you . . . His peace. A preview of the supernatural activity He's preparing for you to experience.

When you have His peace concerning a specific situation—that does not contradict the edicts of His written Word and has been continually strengthened by the "mercy of confirmation"—you should begin to consider that you're hearing His voice.

Peace and truth are the great subject matter of divine revelation . . . truth to direct us, peace to make us easy.

—Matthew Henry

Peace Rules

"Peace" is one of those concepts that comes to us wrapped in all kinds of cultural packaging. "Peace" can have sort of an airy, dreamy, wistful feel. But when we talk about the peace of God, don't think of singing and swaying and holding hands in a circle. The peace of God is strong, intense, palpable, real. You can sense its stable presence giving you inner security despite insecure circumstances.

And it's ours.

Bought by Christ's blood and suffering.

When you accepted Him as your Lord and Savior, peace was among the great gifts you received from God Himself, from *Jehovah Shalom* (The Lord is Peace). And as you grow in your relationship with Him, learning how to hear His voice and respond in obedience, peace becomes one of your determining factors in knowing when He is leading and speaking to you. Peace is not only an element of His character; it's evidence of His presence. So even when He tells you to step out in faith, doing something that seems impossible or illogical, His peace comes along as your traveling companion. You may not feel confident in your own ability to do what He's asking. You may not be able to see the outcome it will produce or the details of how to get there. But you feel confident about His Word that He has persistently confirmed, and that will be enough.

When God speaks, you will feel a surety about His word to you and the benefits of being obedient to it.

You'll feel a peace about it.

Think of it as getting a "green light."

Have you ever sat at an intersection where the lights weren't working, perhaps flashing a blinking red or yellow? How did you feel about inching out into the oncoming traffic, knowing the signal above you was indicating caution and careful awareness? But if that same light were to turn a steady green, you'd feel confident in following what the traffic indicator was telling you to do.

You'd have a peace about it.

It's the same way in hearing from God. As you sense His leading, ask yourself, "Am I sensing a 'green light' in my spirit? Am I confident and at peace about moving forward, *even if* I don't like what I'm being compelled to do? Or do I instead feel restless and unsteady, unsure about what these directions are telling me?" Remember, it's imperative that you take time to differentiate between what you might think about your ability, your preferences, or the outcome of the situation, and what you believe about Him and His Word. When God speaks, you may not feel a peaceful steadiness about yourself or your circumstances, but you will feel a surety about His word to you and the benefits of being obedient to it. So it is possible not to prefer or care for the very thing you are certain God has asked you to do. In that case, you move forward in obedience to and dependence on the Lord.

If it's God, you should sense peace in His command despite what lies ahead.

In the New Testament city of Colossae, believers struggled at times with decisions about how to follow God's will in keeping the church strong. Sometimes a sin issue would erupt and they didn't know how to handle it; sometimes they were tempted to treat each other differently because of their ethnic backgrounds; and people came around from time to time with all kinds of weird ideas about what true spirituality looked like and how the Colossians should act. To help, Paul told them, "Let the peace of Christ rule in your hearts to which indeed you were called into one body. . . ." The Greek word for "rule" is significant. It means to act as a judge or umpire. So Paul was telling the church that in the same way a modern day baseball umpire manages a game according to the rules, the Holy Spirit was to serve as the "umpire of their hearts," and the Colossians were to make decisions in accordance with His calls. Christ wanted the Colossians to be committed to and ruled by the assurance given or not given by His Spirit as they sought to discern God's will. In other words, His peace wasn't supposed to be merely a part of their lives; it was to rule them, direct them, and govern everything they did.

When peace reigns in a matter we're dealing with—when God's voice is accompanied by deep assurance and permission—pay close attention to what you're hearing and sensing. You may be wrestling with a decision about a job offer in another city—or an employee you need to hire. Maybe you're trying to decide on which contractor to use for some remodeling work on your house or how to approach a friend who seems to be straying into sin. Perhaps it's a complete career change toward something you've thought about before but have never felt released to actively pursue. Maybe it's a ministry position at church that you admit you feel unqualified for, but you think God might be leading you to accept—or a major purchase you've been studying and researching. It could be any number of things.

See which option is accompanied by a steady, solid, gripping settledness deep within, despite the difficulties you may face if you proceed.

I want to be certain that I am clear about this fact: as believers, we can never lose the God-given peace that accompanies our salvation. It's ours eternally, perpetually. But in the ball game of daily life, the Spirit is making calls for us all the time that we can hear and sense in our own spirit. If we're contemplating something that isn't pleasing to God, His peace will not rule. If we're heading down a path—in life, with the kids, in marriage, in business—and we're wandering *even by accident* out of the path He's set for us, His peace will not rule. If we're moving forward prematurely and ahead of His timing, His peace will not rule. Even with ultimate peace in Christ concerning our relationship to Him as a son or a daughter, we won't at that moment have peace in terms of this particular circumstance.

Don't take lightly those decisions and plans the Spirit rejects. He is steering you back from a cliff of spiritual, financial, or relational danger. He is nudging you away from an experience you think you want, but it isn't even close to what He has in mind for you if you'll just hold on and wait for His word to be confirmed, giving you peace to move forward. (Sometimes, of course, there's not time for indecision, and you are required to make an immediate decision on an important matter. We'll address these kinds of time-sensitive issues in an upcoming chapter.)

So when you feel a contest of wills ensuing in your heart—an uneasiness that makes you think twice about something (sometimes the need to get too many people's opinions is an indicator of this uneasiness)—that's the time to practice the first of the "five Ms." Look for the *message* of the Spirit. Tune in to His peace signal. See if it's there. Find out if He's dispatching assurance and confidence that's working itself up through your mind, will, and emotions, even to your physical senses. If you're really not sure what to do, that alone is probably enough to tell you not to do anything yet.

When it comes to discerning His voice, always remember . . .

Peace rules.

A reigning sense of God's peace confirms His voice to me.
There may have been turmoil getting to that peace, but when I
have settled in on His desire for me, I am assured of that by the
peace that accompanies it.

—Kay Arthur

Peaceful Relations

The indicator of peace is not only good for individuals who want to discern God's will, but also for the collective body of Christ as well. In addition to filling your heart with an internal peace as He leads you toward choosing options and making decisions, also expect the voice of God to direct you into peaceful relationships with others. As you seek to discern what He's saying to you, be cautious about following up on any inclination that's likely to cause division or to impede the spiritual growth of a fellow believer.

Here's a good example of this. In college I belonged to a wonderful Christian sorority, whose goal was to provide an alternative for young women who didn't want to be involved in secular organizations of this type. And I very much enjoyed my time in this group. Good friends. Good experiences.

But I decided that I wanted to be part of another sorority on campus. And I didn't see why this should be anybody's call to make but mine. I knew that many of the girls in our Christian sorority genuinely believed that joining a more traditional one would be displeasing to God. But I believed that the Lord had given me the freedom to do it.

So I did.

Let me just say that the effect of my decision on the girls in my Christian social club was . . . significant. Feelings were hurt. Questions were raised. Concerns were expressed. I was totally taken aback by their reaction. The worst part was that many of the girls were fledgling believers, and these were the ones who struggled the most to make sense of what I'd done.

I didn't really understand it at the time. But looking back from the distance of years and hopefully with a little bit of accumulated wisdom, I now see the problem. Although God had indeed given me personal freedom in that one particular area, my decision to exercise that freedom had caused other Christians to stumble. I should have recognized the discord that my actions would cause, and taken this as my cue not to move forward.

The apostle Paul took up this matter in the book of Romans when dealing with one of the more contentious issues in the early church—whether or not it was all right for Christians to eat food that had been offered to idols. Paul taught that Christians had the liberty to follow their own conscience in this matter, but he also pointed to a deeper issue:

> Let us aim for harmony in the church and try to build each
> other up. Don't tear apart the work of God over what you eat.
> Remember, all foods are acceptable, but it is wrong to
> eat something if it makes another person stumble. It is
> better not to eat meat or drink wine or do anything else
> if it might cause another believer to stumble.
> Romans 14:19–21 NLT

Your relationship with family, friends, church members, and coworkers is more than just a natural kinship, more than just people you hang out with. These fellow believers, especially those who are closest and dearest, have been entrusted to you. You bear a responsibility toward them. So before you "do anything else," as Paul said, think of how your actions will affect them, because pursuing peace and building each other up are much more important than your personal freedoms.

The Holy Spirit will not lead us to do anything that in any way hinders the peace and unity in the body.

Now I want to be sure you don't hear me saying something that often gets miscommunicated when this subject comes up. I'm not saying that you should only do what people approve of. If you're not careful, the Enemy can turn a legitimate concern about edifying your fellow believers into a form of bondage. If you're not being discerning, the constant pressure of worrying about how your decisions and lifestyle will affect others can keep you from enjoying the freedoms legitimately given to you by God.

So this idea of not causing another believer to "stumble" is a major element in living this out. In order for someone to stumble, they first have to be moving forward, right? Moving is a prerequisite for stumbling to occur. Therefore, in terms of this discussion, what you need to be most concerned about is not society in general, or even other Christians who are only nominally practicing their faith. Your concern should be not to impede the progress of other believers who are *moving*—who are growing spiritually in a vibrant relationship with Christ.

These are the kinds of people who have done more than merely accept Christ as Savior. They have clearly demonstrated they are on a journey with God, moving forward in their relationship—eager and growing and going to the next level. These were the people that the young women in my Christian sorority were—girls who loved the Lord and were truly seeking Him. For me to join a secular club, when I knew this was an issue they were wrestling with, showed a disregard for their spiritual progress and self-centeredness in my own heart over this particular matter. I became a stumbling block to them because my decision had a hand in shaking their young, active faith and their confidence in God.

A little thing? Maybe. But it caused harm, and it did not honor Christ. It wasn't built on peace.

Peaceable relationships are vitally important to God. Therefore, we can conclude that the Holy Spirit will not lead us to do anything that in any way hinders the peace and unity in the body. This doesn't mean everyone will agree with what you're doing, but it does mean your decision will not cause another believer to stumble or bring massive division within the body of Christ.

God's voice speaks the language of peace.

So when He opens your eyes to see that another follower of Christ will be hurt by what you're about to do, what He's saying to you is, "Not now!" This doesn't mean you've lost your freedom entirely or forever. You're just not supposed to exercise and enjoy it right then and there. Preserving a fellow Christian from stumbling trumps your personal freedom.

Here's the question to ask yourself: "I know there are some who may not agree with me, but if I do this, is there anyone whose spiritual growth will be hindered by my choice?" If there is, then wisely choose to forgo your freedom for now. Encourage their spiritual growth.

It's the peaceful thing to do, and God will honor you for doing it.

> The wisdom from above is first pure, then peaceable, gentle, reasonable, full of mercy and good fruits, unwavering, without hypocrisy. And the seed whose fruit is righteousness is sown in peace by those who make peace.
> James 3:17–18

Go in Peace

A civil war rages within us as the still unsanctified parts of our souls fight to fulfill the lusts of the flesh. Unbelievers, of course, can't help themselves. As long as they remain resistant to Christ and outside of His redemptive covenant, they will always be at war with themselves and ultimately lack the peace that only God can give.

But we as believers in Christ—we can hear the voice of the Holy Spirit echoing within us, leading us by His peace and calling us to peace with our brothers and sisters.

Internal peace. External peace.

You'll know it's the voice of God when His persistent, personal word to you leaves you with a sense of peace and assurance all the way around.

Chapter Challenges

- When determining God's will, ask Him for confirmation that leads to an internal sense of peace.

- If at all possible, resist the urge to move forward prematurely when you lack peaceful assurance.

- You can feel assurance about His word without being confident in your ability or your circumstances. Be careful to differentiate one from the other.

- God's directions will not encourage you to do something that causes another believer to stumble or produces unnecessary division.

HE WILL CHALLENGE YOU *Chapter Eight*

The gate is narrow and the way
is hard that leads to life.

Matthew 7:14 ESV

*M*y son stared intently at the cocoon dangling from a bush beside our house. For days he'd been watching the tiny structure, looking for changes and activity, eagerly awaiting the moment when the emperor moth would finally emerge.

Today seemed to be the day.

The cocoon rocked and shook as we watched the tiny insect struggle to free itself from the confines of its silken shell. Fascinating.

After what seemed like an eternity (ten minutes), he started to get frustrated and impatient waiting for this hatching process to complete, and he begged me to do something that would help this little guy make his exit.

I had been so excited about the cocoon since it was a chance to give Jackson a firsthand lesson in nature. But I was even more excited now as this teachable moment appeared, the chance to give my son a firsthand lesson in life—a lesson that penetrated my own heart as well, even as I spoke it.

"You see, Son, it's important for the moth to struggle like this, or else it'll never be able to reach its full potential," I told him. "Unless it builds itself up by battling its way out of the cocoon, it'll never develop that beautiful wingspan or the leg strength to survive. If it gets out too early, without fighting through, it'll be crippled the rest of its life."

The challenge is part of the plan.

We knew that, didn't we?

Or maybe we'd forgotten. Or didn't want to admit it. But since our heavenly Father's goal is to help us reach our full spiritual potential as believers in Christ, we too will often be challenged by the things He calls us to do.

Sometimes *really* challenged.

And it won't be a mistake or a divine mishap. It will be on purpose.

This is God's time-honored track record. He has always called people from unlikely places, asking them to do things that were far beyond their abilities, far beyond what they felt equipped to handle. In fact, if you want to get really honest about it, this pattern seems to be the most consistent way to characterize God's voice in Scripture. Over and over again, He laid down a challenge.

When God spoke . . .

- Noah was asked to build an ark.
- Abraham was asked to leave home for an unknown country.
- Gideon was asked to go to battle with less than adequate troops.
- Samuel was asked to give a tough message to his mentor, Eli.
- Esther was asked to plead the case for her people before a king.
- Mary was asked to become the mother of the Messiah.

I could go on, but for some reason I just don't think I have to. I'm sure you're doing a good job of filling in the blanks right from where you're sitting, drawing mental images from your own personal experience—times when the task God has set before you has completely and utterly alarmed you. There was no way you were going to accomplish in your own power what He was asking you to do. So maybe you tried to avoid it or thought it couldn't possibly be God when He knows good and well that *you* don't have what it takes to see *that* through to the end. Right?

Not so much. This is God's way. Putting extraordinary tasks on the plates of ordinary people so that ordinary people can see what an extraordinary God can do through them.

God's purposes are always higher than ours. They go beyond our natural abilities and thought processes. Yes, what He's saying to you may sound impossible. But if you'll just follow Him in stunned, submitted obedience, stepping out of your cozy comfort zone, you'll find you're leaving the realm of your natural abilities behind and entering the realm of His supernatural ones.

So what'll it be?

Up for a challenge?

If what you sense from God never contains anything that surprises you, you're probably making it up yourself.

—Jan Johnson

Through Many Dangers

I've got to be honest with you—this characteristic of God's voice has become the primary way that I recognize His leading in my life. It's been a pattern in His dealings with me. When I look back at where He has taken me in ministry, every stage of it has been built on one challenging message from God after another. At every single point when our ministry moved from one level to another, there was a sturdy bridge of challenge we had to cross to get there. Most often I've been afraid—highly intimidated—by what the Lord was telling me to do. But when I've moved forward, often only by the encouragement of my spouse or other godly friends, I've been astounded by the outcome and by what I've learned in the process. I've learned—and am still learning—that when I find myself in situations like these, the mere fact that I'm being asked to accomplish something beyond my natural power is often my cue to move forward. But here's the thing: whenever I've just gone along with Him, He has never failed to show up right on time, giving me exactly what I need. I may not always agree with His plans initially, but I am learning to trust Him anyway.

I'll tell you where I've often felt this reality most acutely. As someone who does a lot of public speaking, I am meticulous about the preparation I put in. Through lots of prayer and study, I feel like I get a good understanding of what a particular audience needs to hear. So by the time I arrive at an engagement, ready to minister, I am fully aware of what my message will be.

I've learned, however, not to tell anyone else ahead of time what I'm planning to talk about, because more than once the Lord has decided to change things up on me. Hours before, sometimes *minutes* before I'm ready to take the platform, He will impress on me the need to address an entirely different topic. Based on what He's been doing at the event, He leads me in another direction than the one I'd been planning to go.

Whew—that's scary. As if I'm not nervous enough already about standing before hundreds or thousands of people, hoping I remember everything I'd prepared to say, now I'm being told through that inner voice, that inner nudge of God's Spirit, to basically go out there and wing it.

But I can testify to you from firsthand experience that every time I've responded to that Holy Spirit inclination, every time I've thrown myself headlong into His power and anointing, it hasn't been comfortable, but the words have come. Maybe not as fluently or articulately as I would have preferred, but they've come. And instead of just being my well-planned words, they were *His* words, flowing strongly and supernaturally through a person who could not have done that on her own. God gives me the courage. God gives me the power. And I kick at another little piece of that cocoon until, wouldn't you know it, I'm flying on the wings of His supernatural strength.

That is the purpose behind His challenge—to put us in position to see the miraculous work of His power operating in our frailty.

And that is the purpose behind His challenge—to put us in position to see the miraculous work of His power operating in our frailty.

And this is what we say we want. We pray to experience God's miracles, to see Him show us a sign of His goodness. But then we dodge and duck and do everything possible to keep from being put into a place where miracles are most likely to occur: in the tight spots, the dead ends, out on the limbs where the only way to go is down, and God is the only one able to catch us.

Jeremiah is a case in point. He was just a young man when God called him to be His spokesman, and he knew the job was too much for him. "Alas, Lord God! Behold, I do not know how to speak, because I am a youth" (Jeremiah 1:6). He was scared to death to accept God's challenging assignment.

But the Lord answered him, "Do not say, 'I am a youth,' because everywhere I send you, you shall go, and all that I command you, you shall speak. Do not be afraid of them, for I am with you to deliver you" (verses 7–8).

Jeremiah heard from God and accepted His challenge. Stepped out in obedience. Proclaimed the words that God put in his mouth. Told the people of Judah exactly what would happen to them if they didn't repent of their sins and turn back to God: the Babylonians would come and destroy Jerusalem and carry them all away into captivity.

I'm not saying that everything went great for Jeremiah just because he was faithful to do what God had told him. He went through more than he thought he was capable of enduring, yet God gave a naturally timid man the courage to persevere in the face of severe persecution. He gave him the word of the Lord to declare for more than forty years. He did something supernatural in an ordinary life.

That's the purpose behind His challenge—to allow His children to see His power in the challenge.

What about Moses? The outstanding accomplishments of his life began with an extremely challenging message from God—to return to the very place where he had fled for his life as a younger man, "so that you may bring My people, the sons of Israel, out of Egypt" (Exodus 3:10).

Moses was nearly eighty by this time. He'd finally found peace and a family and a fair chance of dying a natural death one day in a comfortable place, at a ripe old age. So when he first heard this plan of God for his life,

Moses didn't start off by saying, "Sure, God, no problem. I'll just run down there, spring the people out, and then get back here to my day job."

He couldn't *believe* what God was asking. He was completely overwhelmed. When God called him to lead this rescue operation, Moses protested, "I can't do it! I'm such a clumsy speaker! Why should Pharaoh listen to me?" (Exodus 6:30 NLT). But the Lord said, "Pay close attention to this. I will make you seem like God to Pharaoh" (Exodus 7:1 NLT).

Moses. Just a man with a hard calling. But the challenge presented the opportunity for him to represent God in a generation-defining moment.

That's the purpose behind God's challenge.

In other words, God has always wanted to supernaturally equip His people for challenging tasks, allowing the power of the Almighty to be manifested through them.

And it's the same with us. When we willingly submit to the Lord's challenges—despite our shock, fear, and hesitancy—we release the splendors of the Almighty to be seen in us.

That's the purpose behind His challenge. Always has been and always will be.

> Have you ever heard the Master say something very difficult to you? If you haven't, I question whether you have ever heard Him say anything at all.
>
> —Oswald Chambers

Easy Doesn't

Interesting, isn't it, that the teaching of this chapter comes on the heels of our talking about God's voice being characterized by "peace." *So which is it? When I'm trying to hear God speak, do I expect a sense of His peace, or do I wait for Him to scare the living daylights out of me?*

Let me just say there's a difference between peace and comfort, between internal accord and external ease. *Peace* is not a weak, passive word. *Peace,* in God's dictionary, is more like an action verb.

And with trust comes peace.

Even amid challenge.

So don't confuse following God's will with agreeing with it. He desires to show His strength in you, and He will encourage you to do things that require great faith and trust in Him and in His work for you.

The peaceful way is not the same as the easy way. And while I'm not suggesting that God's word to you will never be an easy task (Naaman's encounter with the prophet Elisha in 2 Kings 5 illustrates that), I *am* saying that when you sense something particularly challenging, you shouldn't discount it as not being from God. When you have a strong conviction that points you in a difficult direction, your spiritual ears should perk up in God's direction. Alternative sources would rarely encourage you to tap into God's divine resources or inspire you to have a more complete dependence upon the Lord.

Let me tell you who seems to enjoy championing the "easy way." Let's go back to the wilderness of Matthew 4, where the Lord Jesus had been led "by the Spirit" (verse 1)—don't miss *that* little point—to endure a challenging forty-day fast in preparation for the ministry He was set to embark on.

Along came Satan with enticements for Jesus to turn stones into bread (to ease His hunger), to perform an astonishing public miracle (to get people's attention), and to bow down to His Enemy in exchange for worldly power and influence (to avoid God's plan—including, of course, the suffering and death).

With each new statement, the Enemy's voice encouraged Jesus to do what would have been easier for Him in His current situation. To a man who hadn't eaten in more than a month, turning stones into bread would sound like a pretty good idea. Proving His supernatural abilities and flaunting His power by commanding the angels to catch His spectacular fall would *He* wants to challenge you . . . to show you what He can do when you admit you can't.

have made Him look like a superstar, thrilling an eager audience.

Between Satan's voice and the voice of our own flesh and ego, we can be sure of hearing an easier way to get around God's challenging way, and it will have a much nicer ring to it.

But that's often how we can differentiate between God's voice and the voice of a "stranger" (John 10:5).

By the challenge.

When you need to resolve an argument with your spouse, the easy way is to blast your opinions immediately. The challenging way is to keep quiet and take the matter to the Lord.

When you're waiting for someone to make a decision, the easy way is to call and pester and force a deadline. The challenging way is to stay patient and prayerful and do something productive with the meantime.

We are often tempted to do the opposite of what God asks us to do simply because it's easier. But doing the easy thing will never stretch you, will never force you to draw on His resources (the very goal He has in mind for you), and will not cause God to be most glorified.

Satan's goal is to keep you in the cocoon—weak, effortless, lazy. He would not ask you to struggle out, and he certainly doesn't want you to experience the fullness of God's power. Your ego, likewise, would not ask you to do anything that might cause you embarrassment or a blow to your self-image. Fear will present an option that keeps you protected and safe instead of inviting you into the risky unknowns of God's will.

- God will say, "Apologize for what you did." Ego says, "Don't worry. Nobody noticed."

- God will say, "Give to that person in need." Fear says, "I've got a huge bill that needs to be paid."

- God will say, "Be respectful to your boss, even though he doesn't deserve it." Your flesh says, "Why should I do that after the way he's treated me?"

- God will say, "Stop participating in that activity." The Enemy says, "Your friends wouldn't understand that."

- God will say, "Allow your husband to lead in that area." You'll say, "I could do it faster and better."

Your Father wants you to experience Him, not just know Him, by allowing you access to see His supernatural activity. He wants you walking by faith, trusting Him to provide, displaying His glory and majesty in ways you could never do yourself. He desires to show you what it looks and feels like to see Him supernaturally fill in the margin that is left when your abilities run out.

He wants to challenge you . . . to show you what He can do when you admit you can't.

So when a thought comes to you out of left field, consider—before you dismiss it—that it might be God's thought for you. Don't just ignore it. Check inward to see if the Holy Spirit is encouraging you to pursue it despite the challenge it presents.

I often know God is speaking when a thought occurs to me that surprises me, maybe makes me a little uncomfortable, and I know it's something I can't do in my own power. When I take a thought like that to the Lord in prayer, when I consult the Word and even godly counsel, and my Holy Spirit–led conscience will not let me rest until I move forward with it, I assume this is God speaking. He now has me right where He wants me—relying on His power, not my own, to do what He's asking.

His challenge is working.

When Henry Blackaby, author of *Experiencing God*, was still in seminary, his church asked him to be their music and education director. Well, that was nice of them to ask, but he had never sung in a choir before or led music of any kind, so he was naturally a little uneasy about taking on a responsibility like that. But as he continued to seek the Lord's will, he felt that God was leading him to accept. So despite his obvious lack of experience, he willingly obeyed.

After successfully serving in this capacity for two years, the church called him to be their pastor, even though he hadn't preached but a handful of sermons and again felt unqualified for the role. Yet when he took this to God in prayer, he again felt led to accept.

That was the beginning of a ministry that has spanned decades and blessed millions of people through his books, his speaking, and his worldwide ministry. But if he'd always chosen the easy way, the comfortable way, he'd never have been in a position to see God's full potential reached in his life, and we would never have benefitted from the extraordinary ministry God has set forth through him.

Not if he'd resisted God's challenge.

The apostle Paul talked about his own feelings of inadequacy and his experiences with how God worked supernaturally through him. He often felt ill-equipped to take on the challenge God was asking. But "each time [God] said, 'My gracious favor is all you need. My power works best in your weakness.'" To which Paul responded, "So now I am glad to boast about my weaknesses, so that the power of Christ may work through me" (2 Corinthians 12:9 NLT).

It's a sure thing. God will provide where He guides. It is better for you to choose the challenging road—if God is in it—than to select the route that is easier and more convenient but lacks the presence and power of God.

No, you don't have what it takes to do it. You're not able. You can't.

But the Spirit is saying He wants to do it through you.

That's one way you know God is speaking.

By the challenge.

Chapter Challenges

- Don't discount an option just because it is the most difficult possibility.

- Remember this: (1) Your ego will present an option designed to keep your self-image intact. (2) Your fear will present the route of safety, free from the risks often required to tap into divine reserves. (3) Your Enemy will offer ease and comfort to keep you from accessing God's supernatural resources. (4) Your flesh will hope to appease itself and satisfy its own desires.

- Peace and challenge can coexist. You can have an internal assurance about God's directives and still encounter external challenge and difficulty.

HE EXUDES TRUTH *Chapter Nine*

The word of the Lord holds true,
and we can trust everything he does.

Psalm 33:4 NLT

*L*et's recall what God sounds like when He speaks:

- He is persistent.
- He speaks personally.
- He brings a sense of peace.
- He often delivers a challenge.

These are the kinds of patterns and messages we're to be looking for when discerning God's voice. But wherever any doubt remains about whether or not you're hearing Him clearly as you listen, as you wait, as you watch for His confirmation, the bottom line is this . . .

He speaks principally through His Word.

And His Word is always true.

When I was little and my mother needed to leave me somewhere for a short period of time, she would always squat down in front of me, look me squarely in the eye, and say, "Priscilla, you stay here until I come back. Don't go with anybody. Don't believe anyone who tells you I sent them to get you. I'm not sending anybody else. You stay right here and wait for me." I had my mother's word on that.

She had made herself abundantly clear. There was no need to question it. If anyone told me anything that went contrary to what she'd said, I would know immediately they weren't telling me the truth, because she had already spoken on that issue, and she would stand behind her word.

The way God stands behind His.

When we read the Scriptures, it's as if He is squatting down in front of us, cupping our face in His hands, and saying, "This is who I am, and this is what I'm going to do. Don't let anybody tell you differently. Don't trust anyone who makes you doubt what I'm saying to you. Believe Me, because I am telling you the truth."

That's why these last two chapters in the section are so crucially important, because everything we've learned up till now about listening for God to speak ultimately rests on the bedrock of God's truth. Anyone who refuses to act on the knowledge He reveals in His Word—and likewise anyone who chooses to act on a gut feeling that goes against His biblical teaching—will never know how to discern His voice.

Where the Scriptures are ignored, He remains the unknown God.

Therefore, the more acquainted you become with the Word, the more accurately you'll be able to hear from Him. The Bible provides the framework into which His messages to you will come. Anything the Spirit says will fall within the boundaries of what has already been written.

So bet your bottom dollar on this guiding principle: You will hear Him most accurately as you remain constant and consistent in your study and meditation of His holy Word.

When He speaks, He speaks the truth.
He is the "God of truth" (Psalm 31:5).

We deceive ourselves if we claim to want to hear His voice but
neglect the primary channel through which it comes. We must
read His Word. We must obey it. We must live it, which means
rereading it throughout our lives.

—Elisabeth Elliot

I'd Know That Voice Anywhere

My brother Anthony Evans Jr. is the spitting image of our father. Not
only does he bear my father's name, but if you were to hear the two of them
speak, you'd notice they sound almost exactly alike—a little trick my brother
has often employed when wanting to have some fun at others' expense. I've
seen him on the phone, pretending to be my dad, talking with even some
very close acquaintances, and pulling off the charade for quite a while before
they realize they're not talking to the man they thought they were.

But that would never work on me. No matter how much alike my
brother's and my father's voices may sound, Anthony can't fool me for a
second. He may be able to pull that stuff on other people, but when I hear
him trying to con me with that impersonation gag of his, he's busted almost
before he starts. I've spent enough time with both him and my dad to know
well the small but distinct differences in their inflections and tones of voice.

The apostle Paul warned us that Satan often disguises himself as an
"angel of light" (2 Corinthians 11:14). He deliberately tries to speak to us
in a way that sounds deceptively akin to the Holy Spirit's voice. But as hard
as he tries to imitate the voice of God, he will never sound exactly like the
real thing. Therefore, the more intimate we become with God and His
Word, the more quickly we'll be able to tell who's really speaking. If we want
to be able to recognize Satan's lies—and who doesn't!—we must be sure
we're spending lots of time in close fellowship with the Truth. The more we
read the written Word, the more acquainted we become with God's character, personality, patterns, and ways. When God speaks today, His voice

will carry the same personality and patterns, and will reveal the same attributes as He reveals in His Word. We'll know His voice because it will "sound" like the One we've come to know so well in the Scriptures.

It's like the difference between the stiff, reserved conversation of a stranger you've just been introduced to and the familiar chatting of a close friend with whom you've shared years of life and memories and common relationships.

People will often say something like, "I think I'm hearing from God, but I'm just not sure. What if it's the Enemy luring me into a huge mistake? What if it's just my own voice, leading me in the direction of what I truly want and prefer? How can I know if it's God or not?"

The Lord wants your relationship with Him to be so close that Satan's voice can never deceive you. He wants you close enough that upon receiving a certain impression, you can know if it lines up with the nature of the God you've come to know so well through the Scriptures. Then when what you are sensing seems strange, you can confidently say, "My God would never say anything like that." If you focus on the priority of knowing Him and knowing His Word, discernment will start to happen automatically, on its own.

You'll know whether or not you're hearing from Him because you've grown so close to Him.

Paul's example teaches us about the importance and primacy of knowing Him. The very first thing Paul asked when he met the risen Savior on the road to Damascus was, "Who are You, Lord?" (Acts 9:5). And by the time God had more fully answered that question for him through many years of challenge, experience, and intimate relationship, the apostle could declare, "Everything else is worthless when compared with the infinite value of knowing Christ Jesus my Lord. For his sake I have discarded everything else, counting it all as garbage, so that I could gain Christ" (Philippians 3:8 NLT).

> *If* we've not taken care of the basics, we shouldn't anticipate any fruit.

Nothing, Paul said, is as wonderful as knowing Christ—not even hearing His voice and knowing His will, as precious as those are. Hearing Him and discerning His direction were never Paul's primary goal because he fully understood that if he knew Him, all those other things would naturally follow.

I want to be sure you don't miss this—the singular importance of knowing God—the key to knowing His voice. Pause for a moment and take a little personal inventory.

- Could it be that you're having trouble discerning God's voice because you've somehow bypassed the need to know who He really is?
- Have you been "voice hunting" more than "God hunting"?
- Has knowing His will taken precedence over just knowing Him?

I've asked questions like these of myself numerous times over the years. Still do, in fact. Like you, what I've often wanted to know most from God are the details—where He wants me to go, what He wants me to do, even what He wants to do for me! I've been guilty of seeking God's direction and blessing more than I seek Him. I can't tell you how many times His tender conviction—the kind that comes only from God—has told me that my focus was on the wrong thing. It's like trying to grow a nice, tall apple tree with blossoming leaves and luscious ripe apples when you've not planted a seed. If you've not taken care of the basics, you shouldn't anticipate any fruit. To expect otherwise is absurd.

When knowing God is our chief priority, He will reveal truths about Himself—His personality and His plans—that will point us toward the path we should take. Then when we take it, we'll be able to walk ahead carrying the greatest blessing of all—the privilege of close, warm relationship with God. When His presence is our constant companion, His chosen path not only becomes clearer to us, it also becomes the only path we truly want.

King David seemed to have a handle on this priority. We know from Scripture that he endured many distressing circumstances and disappointments throughout his lifetime. Many members of his own family denigrated him (see 1 Samuel 17:28; 2 Samuel 6:20). His predecessor, King

Saul, tried on more than one occasion to kill him. David later fell hard into a deep pit of sin, experiencing a season of self-imposed distance from God. Even as king, he watched the wicked prospering while God's people were floundering.

Yet despite all of this, he could say to the Lord, "With all my heart I have sought You" (Psalm 119:10). His focus was not primarily on his circumstances or what he expected God to do about them. His focus was on God Himself. He never became so disillusioned by his problems and pitfalls that he stopped seeking to know God. Even when he felt as if God was no longer speaking, and he couldn't figure out why, the consuming passion of his heart was still to follow hard after Him.

You'll know you're seeking something other than God Himself when you're in one of those in-between stages of life—when nothing seems to be happening and God doesn't seem to be speaking to you in a voice you can clearly discern—and you start to trail away from Him. Or when you're facing a particularly trying time, and you stop pursuing Him. If you no longer seek Him with "all your heart" when things get difficult, this is an indication that you're more interested in what you expect Him to do for you than in simply knowing Him.

And knowing Him is how hearing Him happens.

Knowing Him is how you recognize His truth.

> Whoever seeks God as a means toward desired ends will not find God. The mighty God, the maker of heaven and earth, will not be one of many treasures, not even the chief of all treasures. He will be all in all, or He will be nothing.
>
> —A. W. Tozer

One God, One Truth

While Jesus was ministering on earth, He frequently punctuated His teaching with "I'm telling you the truth." Those who heard Him knew that what He was saying was not an opinion or a proposal but was fact. Pure truth. And as Jesus prepared to depart the earth and return to His Father,

He assured His confused, concerned disciples, "When He, the Spirit of truth comes, He will guide you into all the truth" (John 16:13).

The Greek word for "truth" in this verse denotes a "two plus two equals four" kind of truth. Truth with absolutely no mixture of bias, pretense, falsehood, or deceit. When you hear the voice of the Holy Spirit, you can be certain that what He says is the truth, the whole truth, and nothing but the truth. It will always line up with Scripture, the foundation of truth.

The Holy Spirit who lives within you will never speak to you without having received direct revelation from God. He doesn't create messages on His own initiative. "Whatever He hears, He will speak; and He will disclose to you what is to come" (verse 13). Every message He delivers to you comes straight from the God of truth.

So not only do we need to know the Scripture because we can get to know God, but also because we can get to know His standard that He will never compromise in His personal word to us.

The Holy Spirit—the only One with direct access to the truth of God's thoughts concerning you—also has a desire to share divine revelations with you. He'll do it in a vast number of ways (as we've discussed before), but His message to you will always be solidly based on what He's already revealed in His Word. You won't be left to create your own standard of truth, building it from some compound blend of personal tastes, postmodern culture, and human traditions. Which is exactly what a friend of mine I'll call Cooper did.

He had decided to leave his wife. When he told me his reasons, my patience grew thin. By taking Scriptures out of context and applying them inappropriately, he had woven a web of rationalizations to justify his actions. Now with great self-assurance—the kind we're able to cobble together in private with long hours of Satan's deceptive help, talking ourselves into whatever position we ultimately want to land on—he tried to elicit my approval.

He was certain he'd heard from God. Positive. He'd determined, in fact, that God was not only allowing him this option but was actually prepared to bless his union with another person who made him "happy."

As I listened, I thought back to the many years of spiritual fruit his salvation had produced. Knowing that the Holy Spirit truly lived in him, I had a hard time grasping how he could have drifted so far off base when it came to discerning God's voice.

But that's what was happening. He had chosen to take a particular course of action, and now he'd capped it off by convincing himself that he'd received God's stamp of approval.

Yet even though he may have *felt* led to do this, I can guarantee you the Holy Spirit wasn't the one leading him. He could not have heard the Spirit of truth, because He speaks only what He hears from God (John 16:13). And God never speaks contrary to His written Word.

Never.

But I shouldn't really have been all that surprised. We've all been in a position like this at one time or another, haven't we? We thought for certain God was telling us something specific. We knew it. We were sure of it. The only place we got a little fuzzy was when we tried squaring it with what we knew of Scripture, or when we tried explaining our thinking to a parent or friend who lived on intimate terms with God. Then it took a lot of mental effort and self-styled logic to try holding all the loose ends together. The voice we thought we'd heard from God didn't fare so well in the light of His Word. We were left to determine: Will we count on God's Word as truth? Will we choose to conform to His true character despite what we are feeling?

This is what Cooper had to contend with. He was substituting cultural norms for God's truth. As we talked, I discovered that most of the couples in his family had left their spouses for trivial reasons and remarried. He had learned this behavior as a child and grown comfortable with it over time. So my husband and I tried to help him realize that no matter how deeply his family history and patterns of behavior were woven into the fabric of his life, they still didn't override God's truth. Whenever these two strong forces collide in opposition to one another, God's Word is the horse you want to ride out on.

I understand how predisposed we are to view cultural and family practices with something close to religious fervor, letting them trump anything that threatens to challenge them. We see this in the life of the early church, as those who'd been raised according to Jewish culture bristled at what God was doing in uniting Jews and Gentiles under the lordship of Christ.

One of the more controversial issues of this dynamic, as mentioned before, was the debate over acceptable foods. According to Jewish tradition, certain foods were okay to eat and others were not. But when Christ came, He allowed His followers to eat foods that had previously been considered unclean. He clarified that they were free to experience life with Him without focusing primarily on externals.

But they didn't acquiesce to this all at once. When Jewish believers found themselves in fellowship with Gentile believers, who did not have the same dietary restrictions in their background, the conviction of tradition and culture clashed with that of their new brothers and sisters. One day, while dining with some Gentile believers, Peter found himself rather enjoying the unity God had brought to these Christ-centered relationships by allowing them to share their meals together. But when some pals from his old neighborhood showed up and saw what their buddy Peter was doing, the heartburn of cultural tradition sort of caught in his throat. He could feel their stares and condescension. Being surrounded by people who shared with him a common ancestry and way of thinking caused him to distance himself from the Gentiles, ignoring them in deference to a tug of tradition.

Boy, the apostle Paul turned red-hot on that. Once a strict legalist himself, he saw exactly what was happening and knew well what was going on in Peter's head. And he aimed to nip this issue in the bud "in the presence of all" (Galatians 2:14). With the blunt force of his powerful words, he let Peter know he was not being "straightforward about the truth of the gospel." Peter was letting tradition shape his thinking, rather than the steady drumbeat of God's consistent Word.

It can be so easy for us to lean on our own understanding, to assume it's okay for us to let our cultural compass be what determines the choices we make. But God's standard of truth is often very different from the one our family, our tradition, perhaps even our church denomination teaches. Just because we feel comfortable doing something, or just because we have an internal impression that lines up with the other characteristics we've already discussed in previous chapters, doesn't necessarily make it right. We must filter everything through God's revealed truth.

His Word.

Always go back to His Word.

Anything you hear that contradicts Scripture is not from Him.

If you're currently struggling with a decision, confused as to whether the voice you're hearing is coming from the Spirit of Truth or not, ask yourself . . .

- Will it contradict the truth found in Scripture?
- Will it cause me to indulge in sin of any kind?
- Will it encourage me to hypocritically cover up my sin?
- Will it give glory to God by magnifying His truth to the people involved?

When filtered through the truth of God's Word and His Spirit, His voice starts coming clear. We're able to know—to *know*—that we're acting according to the will of God.

> We have received, not the spirit of the world,
> but the Spirit who is from God, so that we may
> know the things freely given to us by God.
> I Corinthians 2:12

Breaking Down Strongholds

Let's look at one more extremely critical reason for staying committed to the truth of God's Word: strongholds. Scripture is the mechanism we use to demolish these chief barriers to hearing from God.

Strongholds are spiritual barricades that keep the voice of God from reaching our spiritual ears. Paul called them "fortresses," "speculations," and "lofty things" that become set up in our hearts "against the knowledge of God" (2 Corinthians 10:4–5).

Against the truth.

Strongholds are things like worry. Fear. Unforgiveness. Low self-esteem. Pride. Doubt. Cynicism. Sin. Ideas and thought processes that run counter to and take priority over the truth of God's thoughts, eventually manifesting themselves in our actions.

Granted, we have contributed to the presence of these intruders in our lives. Even if they were born as the result of others' sin and mistreatment of us, we have been complicit in cooperating with the Devil's purposes in building structures like these inside of us. But let's be clear about this: strongholds are Satan's handiwork.

There is an Enemy of your soul, my friend, and he is in the business of stronghold construction. He may not be able to snatch you from the Father's hand, but he is bent on doing everything devilishly possible to keep you from hearing God's voice, believing the truth, and experiencing the abundant life you've been saved to live.

Remember the diagrams in chapter 2 that show our human makeup as body, soul, and spirit? And how the presence of the Holy Spirit at the core

of our being, which occurs at salvation, begins radiating truth through our soul structure of mind, will, and emotion, changing us from the inside out?

Well, check *this* out. This is what happens to that process of sanctification as strongholds develop in our soul.

Just having these spiritual cancers inside us is bad enough. But as these fortresses of doubt and rebellion barricade God's truth, the Spirit's work in us is hindered, preventing us from hearing clearly or even at all. Eventually the presence of Satan's lies festering at soul level manifests itself outwardly through our system, showing up in our body. Though created with evil intention by the Devil, these distortions grow and multiply as we feed and strengthen them, allowing them to grow into towers of resistance.

This is the source of physical addictions and eating disorders, of unhealthy relationships and sexual immorality. Strongholds have been erected against the truth of God, and therefore our lives bear the strain and even showcase the evidence of the Devil's deception.

If this describes you—and at times it describes most of us—if you're eager to hear the voice of God and are tired of hearing the sound muffled against the brick walls of Satan's lies, let me tell you what I've learned from God's Word and from personal experience. There's only one way to successfully deal with a stronghold.

Demolish it.

We tend to think we should just live with these things. Work around them. Learn to cope with them. We want to believe our reputation and personal influence can survive them, that a new plan will put us in better control of them, that the latest self-help book has the information and strategies we need to neutralize them.

But spiritual strongholds can only be conquered with spiritual weapons. And I know of a Sword that's up for the job.

Paul talks about destroying these ideas that defy the knowledge of God, not with worldly wisdom and tactics "of the flesh," but rather with "weapons of our warfare" that are "divinely powerful for the destruction of fortresses" (2 Corinthians 10:3–4).

Yes, you heard him right.

Destruction.

When you're dealing with the flesh, you can afford to fight with weapons of the flesh. But when you're fighting in the spiritual realm, only God's divine weapons will do. Ephesians 6:10–20 outlines in vivid detail the spiritual armor that we're to gird ourselves with in order to be prepared for battle. Everything listed in that passage is defensive in nature. All except one. We are to actively wield "the sword of the Spirit, which is the word of God" (verse 17). To demolish Satan's lies and make space for God's truth—and to clearly hear His voice again—we must rely completely on the truths of Scripture.

No more playing around. No more dipping in and out of the Word for occasional snacks of inspiration.

This is serious. Get with it.

Just ask Libby. She had picked up some deep emotional scars as a child. Her father had committed adultery numerous times, then both parents had used Libby and her brother as pawns and weapons to manipulate and hurt each other. She felt abandoned, wronged, unprotected, and unloved. Tortured by low self-esteem and self-doubt—strongholds within her very soul—she developed many destructive problems, including an eating disorder, difficulty with relationships, and a haunting, hovering depression. Even after she'd received Christ, these same troubling expressions continued to get the best of her.

But one day while cleaning up her little four-year-old's bedroom, a wave of holy surrender gripped her heart out of nowhere. She sank to the floor, surrounded by her son's playthings, and cried out to God from a fetal position, knowing the only way out of this cycle of despair was something drastic. Radical.

It was demolition day.

Libby began a rigorous discipline of Scripture memorization. Every hour on the hour, she would repeat the same verse three times—often taking the extra precaution of setting her alarm to remind her. At the end of the week, she would take each written verse and file it away by category and subject matter for future battles.

The first few weeks didn't result in a noticeable change. But as these weeks of intense Scripture immersion began to pile up, hope began to replace Libby's depression. A holy strength began to fill her heart and mind.

She was still experiencing temp-
tation—still does to this day—
but "the lies were quieting and
His truth was ringing loudly," she

The Sword of truth at work.

wrote to me later in an e-mail. "The destructive voices in my head were
replaced by His, and the Prince of Peace claimed my heart. I have continued to live triumphantly in Him since then."

That's the Sword of truth at work.

- When your stronghold says, "God could never love you," the Scripture will say, "That's not true. He loves me with an everlasting love"
  (see Jeremiah 31:3).

- When your stronghold says, "God will never accept you," the Scripture will say, "That's not true. I am accepted because of my relationship with Christ" (see Galatians 2:16).

- When your stronghold says, "You'll never be able to do that," the
  Scripture will say, "That's not true. I can do everything with the help
  of Christ, who gives me the strength I need" (see Philippians 4:13).

If you'll take the time to carefully examine some of the ills and struggles you're facing, you may be able to trace them back to a stronghold your
Enemy has constructed to stand as a barrier against God's voice of truth in
your life. A detrimental relationship may begin with the foundational belief
that "I don't deserve any better." A substance abuse addiction may be trace-
able to a belief that "I can only find peace in a bottle." A weight problem
may have started when you convinced yourself, "I have no self-control."
The Enemy's goal is to keep your life so full of strongholds that you not
only experience outward defeat but are subsequently hampered from having
the internal ability to hear God.

So I say to you, "Get out your sword." Chop. Dice. Thrust. Tear down.
Take "every thought captive to the obedience of Christ" (2 Corinthians
10:5). Overthrow the masquerading authority of strongholds by replacing
Satan's lies with the truths of Scripture. Like Libby, the more you digest His

Word, the more you can expect the destruction of any strongholds that are standing in the way of hearing God clearly.

Yes, God's Word is truth. It *reveals truth* about His personality and character, making us more able to discern His voice from others. It *declares truth,* giving us boundaries into which His present direction will fall. And it *wields truth* as a weapon against anything standing in the way of clear reception. So it's our responsibility to remain consistently immersed in His truth so that we can be prepared to hear and heed His leading in our lives.

When you are filled with self-doubt, unsure what to do, what to think, or who to believe, take comfort in knowing you can count on God's Word. When He speaks, He will do what He says. He won't let you down. He won't make you guess. He won't lead you astray.

You have His Word on that.

Chapter Challenges

- Refocus your aim on knowing Him, as opposed to just knowing His direction for your life.

- Since everything God says today will fall within the boundaries of Scripture, be certain to remain loyal to the study of its precepts.

- Keep coming back to these questions when you're not sure how God is leading you: (1) Will it contradict the truth found in Scripture? (2) Will it cause me to indulge in sin of any kind? (3) Will it encourage me to hypocritically cover up my sin? (4) Will it give glory to God by magnifying His truth to the people involved?

- Strongholds block divine reception. Pinpoint any you may have, and then specifically target them for destruction with the weapons of specifically tailored Scripture.

HE SPEAKS WITH
AUTHORITY *Chapter Ten*

Were not our hearts burning within us while
He was speaking to us on the road, while
He was explaining the Scriptures to us?

Luke 24:32

*I*t was just an ordinary morning. Having my regular quiet time of reading the Bible and praying. Praying a typical prayer. Talking with God
about the details of my daily life, asking Him to keep me focused on His
voice through the day—when all of a sudden, the name of an old friend
dropped into my mind, as if my train of thought had suddenly morphed
into a time machine.

She and I had been close friends for many years, but when children
came along and our lifestyles changed, our paths had sort of drifted apart.
You know how it goes. Even though she still meant a lot to me, it had been
quite a while since I'd seen her.

Funny, then, why she'd be coming to mind now. How nice and nostal-
gic. But let's see, where *was* I? Praying? Oh, yeah—praying. So without
skipping a beat, I switched my mind back to present-tense mode and continued on with the devotional task at hand.

Then—there it was again. Her name. And this time the tail end of a
familiar Bible verse trailed along: ". . . love your neighbor as yourself"

(Matthew 19:19). Assuming the Lord must be bringing her to my attention for some unknown reason, I worked her into my prayer at that
moment, asking God to bless her and her family.

How spiritual of me.

But I wasn't sure what to do with this next thought that raced through
my head—the one that said, *"Call her. She needs you."*

I paused, debating the validity of what I'd just heard. Surely God didn't
want me to bypass my prayer and Bible study time to hop on the phone
with an old friend.

"Call her. She needs you."

This just wasn't going away. Like an anchor securing a boat at sea, these
simple words carried with them a weight I could feel in my soul. Although
the message seemed to be of little significance, the impression it made on
me was truly staggering. Immediately my heart sensed the warm stirring
that so often accompanies the voice of God.

Peace.

Assurance.

Authority.

Do it.

So I got up off my knees, turned down the worship music, located her
phone number, and called.

From the moment she answered, I could tell she sounded rushed and
frustrated, even as we shared our polite "long time, no see" greetings. She
told me her husband was at work, her babysitter had called off sick, and she
was at home with her three small children while trying to perform her full-
time work duties that she did from a home office. And she was staring at a
mound of clean laundry that needed to be matched, hung up, or folded and
put away. So she apologized for reacting to my surprise call like this. She
hoped I understood.

Needless to say, I was no longer unclear on why she'd popped into my
mind that morning. To honor the directive in Matthew 19, I knew exactly
what I should do. I spent the remainder of my regular quiet time on that oh,
so regular morning tending to another family's socks, shirts, and bath towels.
I was amazed at the love of God, who would notice one of His children

struggling to make do, then seek out an ordinary someone like me to come over and help.

And you know what? I might've missed the whole thing if He hadn't spoken to me in such a way that I could hardly help but hear Him, by bringing a short verse of Scripture to life. If the thought I'd entertained in my room that morning had merely been a simple brain function, I could've easily reasoned and rationalized it away. That's what we usually try doing, even when we know it's more than that. But because His message came with such significant force and weight, I didn't have to work hard for it to have a resonating impact on me.

When the Holy Spirit speaks, His voice comes with power and authority.

It hits you deep. It *grips* you. Your heart burns.

It's Him. You know it.

I know that God is speaking when His voice is so powerful that it comforts, heals, instructs, corrects, and gives wisdom in only a few words.
—Pat Ashley

Feel the Burn

When Jesus completed what we now know as the Sermon on the Mount, "the crowds were amazed at His teaching; for He was teaching them as one having authority, and not as their scribes" (Matthew 7:28–29).

These "scribes," indicative of all the other religious leaders of Jesus' day, could only teach what they had been taught by someone else. Their words contained no clout in themselves. These men had to refer to one another's writings and teachings to convince their students of the messages they were trying to convey.

But when Jesus spoke . . . *whew!*

Power. Authority.

It was different.

He needed no references or cue cards to assert the validity of His message. His teaching was self-authenticating, producing amazement in those who heard it. Why? Because it landed on their ears with an authority that could only come from God alone. Repeatedly in Scripture, we see the crowds following Him compelled by His words, so refreshing and irresistible.

So rich with authority.

After His death, in Luke 24, we catch up with two people traveling on the road to Emmaus, talking over the number one current event of their day: the trial, crucifixion, and burial of Jesus. They were so engrossed in conversation that when a stranger approached and joined their discussion, they didn't recognize that He was the very One whose experiences they were talking about.

But later, after Jesus had sat down to dinner with them, revealing Himself as the Christ before miraculously vanishing from their sight, these two thought back and admitted that even at their very first encounter with Him—out on the road, in the heat of the day and the heat of the moment—His voice had stirred an immediate internal reaction within them.

When God speaks, His voice is noticeable by its resonance, depth, and impact. It pulses with a calm, steady force that makes a clear impression on your soul. It is the "burning fire" that the prophet Jeremiah described (20:9); it's the "hammer which shatters a rock" (23:29). Like the disciples on their way to Emmaus, you're moved to stillness as you reflect on what you've seen and heard.

Truly, you can distinguish the voice of God from any other voice by the powerful influence it carries in your soul.

> My heart was hot within me, while
> I was musing the fire burned.
> Psalm 39:3

The Word Made Fresh

But it's more than just a feeling. His authoritative voice is not merely a burning sensation that wakes you in the night, a searing thought that pops into your head. Very often His authoritative voice arrives in conjunction with or wrapped in the context of Scripture.

This, again, is another reason why staying deeply in God's Word is so vital to discerning His voice. The more Scripture you hide in your heart—the more frequently and diligently you read it and reread and meditate on its truths—the more opportunity you give the Holy Spirit to bring it quickly to mind, punctuated at a specific moment with a personalized message for you. You see, the Bible not only provides the boundaries within which everything He says will fall, it is the chief mechanism through which God will speak.

I experienced this on a particular occasion when I'd decided to get a group of my friends some small gifts, not because it was Christmas or some convenient holiday but . . . just because. I love giving gifts. I really thought it would bring a ray of sunlight into the lives of these special women.

Soon after I'd made this decision, however, I happened to be reading in Matthew 6, where Jesus said to His followers, "When you give to someone . . . don't let your left hand know what your right hand is doing. Give your gifts in private, and your Father, who sees everything, will reward you" (verses 3–4 NLT). I had read this passage many times, of course, but not when I was right in the middle of looking for the perfect kind of gifts to "give to someone."

Sometimes we wish for a sign in the heavens painted in bold, primary colors that instantly tells us what to do.

Suddenly this passage of Scripture just laid my heart bare, and the strong, authoritative voice of God began asking me questions that I knew were coming directly from His Spirit to me.

What was my motive in giving these gifts? Did I really just want to do something nice for these girlfriends of mine? Or was it more because I wanted to impress them and draw attention to myself? The "living and active" Word of God was "piercing as far as the division of soul and spirit," discerning the "thoughts and intentions of [my] heart" (Hebrews 4:12).

As I prayed about it, suddenly all the peace I'd felt about setting up this little gift-giving thing just drained out of my life. The Spirit had powerfully convicted me that my flesh had stepped up to the plate, wanting a little recognition and affirmation. At least on this one occasion, my desire to give out these gifts—I could see it clearly now—was a way to take for myself the glory that belongs only to God.

That's the illumination of Scripture. A timeless book that gives specific, relevant, authoritative direction to bless and guide us today. That's more than just powerful—it's supernatural.

Sometimes we wish for a sign in the heavens painted in bold, primary colors that instantly tells us what to do, something miraculous that clearly defines what God's will is. We want lightning in a bottle, but we have lightning in the Bible, in the wondrously beautiful, personally instructive, ever-available treasury of His eternal, living Word.

Author and speaker Jill Briscoe tells the story of being in England, wondering whether she should go into some of the local pubs to talk with the kids who were hanging out in there. She worried about her reputation. Worried what people would think if they saw her walking into an establishment such as that. But while she was debating with herself about what to do, the Spirit suddenly and with authority brought to her mind the passage from Philippians 2 that talks about Jesus making Himself "of no reputation," as the King James Bible puts it. The raw energy of God's Word, speaking directly in regard to her question and situation, communicated with clarity to her soul. It was as if God were saying to her, "What are you worrying about your reputation for? Even *I* didn't do that!"

She knew what to do.

She went.

She'd been captured by His authority.

When you're in the Scripture, you shouldn't only be watching for the "thou shalts" and "thou shalt nots" and checking off your reading plan schedule. Those are important, naturally, but I'm suggesting that there should be a tuning of your spiritual ears to notice the moment when a passage captures your attention in an almost shocking way, drawing your thoughts immediately to a personal circumstance to which it applies. When this happens, God is most likely speaking.

Ask yourself: Why is this verse communicating to me so directly right now? What does it mean? Does God have a reason for putting me in this particular zip code of Scripture on this particular day, when I'm right in the middle of this particular circumstance?

It has taken me an incredible number of years as a Christian to realize this stunning reality that's available for every believer. When God's Word leaps off the page and *grips* you—I mean *stuns* you as though you were awakened from sleep by a thunderclap—don't rush ahead with your Bible reading. Stop right there. Lock on to those words that have already locked eyes with your soul. This isn't some random occurrence or coincidence. It is God Himself speaking through His Word. It is the living Word of God at work.

Speaking with authority.

When a Scripture verse or its message hits you out of nowhere while you're in the middle of your day, don't dismiss it. Trust that the Holy Spirit is at work within you, speaking God's Word to you concerning what He needs you to know at that moment, what He wants your next actions to be.

Every time you open your Bible or sit under its teaching, God gives you His general revelation. But often He may choose to give you a specific message clearly tied to the circumstances you're currently facing. These are like those moments when you're sitting in church, the pastor is delivering a message from the Word, and suddenly you feel as though you're the only person in the room, as though he had gotten up that morning, walked to his study, and decided he wanted to speak directly to you about your circumstance, in front of all these people.

My Bible is full of notes and reminders—with dates written beside passages where the Holy Spirit delivered and specifically revealed the Father's plan to me, completely flooding me in His peace and affirmation, assuring me that He was leading me to follow Him in this exact direction.

Just last week, I was a bit overwhelmed by the pressure I was feeling. There were three—count 'em: one, two, three—specific problems that were pressing in on me. I felt like I was staggering under the weight of the burden of these difficulties and prayed specifically that God would give me the knowledge on how to deal with them and the power to do so. My Bible study reading that particular morning was 2 Chronicles 20:12, where King Jehoshaphat prayed, "O our God . . . we are powerless before this great multitude who are coming against us; nor do we know what to do, but our eyes are on You." I began to feel the soothing

Because the Book is alive, it applies anew and fresh to us in every generation.

comfort of God's Spirit wash over me as this verse became a personal prayer from my own heart and I began to focus my attention on Him as instructed in this passage. Intrigued, I looked back to the beginning of the section of Scripture to read more, and I was quickly captivated by the fact that the "great multitude" Jehoshaphat was praying about was composed of three—that's right—exactly three different armies. I knew God was using His Word to speak directly to me.

We must change our thinking about the Bible if we consider it a stagnant rule book to be consulted by page and paragraph number. It's not just an old book with a lot of theology for us to digest. It's a fact: God is no longer in the business of revealing new doctrine. The canon of Scripture is closed. Yet because the Book is alive, it applies anew and fresh to us in every generation. Author Joyce Huggett put it this way: "Listening to God today is not about 'newness' but about 'nowness'."

God's Word is living. When you read it, you should feel the warmth of His breath rising from the page as the Spirit applies it to your particular situation, regardless of how specific or personal. By reading your Bible with a holy anticipation of hearing the living Word, you invite confirmation of the peace you believe you've been sensing within. You open your heart to receive His counsel and to let His guidance illuminate your next steps. You till up fertile soil for Him to plant a pinpointed message in the deepest regions of your being.

My friend and mentor Anne Graham Lotz once said, "I never make a major decision in life, especially one that will affect another person, before I have received direction from God." Yes, I expected her to say that. I feel conviction that I should expect it of myself. But what penetrated my heart was what she told me next—that for every major decision she's made in life, there's a specific Scripture verse she can point to as the one that God used to personally direct her. "When circumstances would have made me doubt a decision," she said, "His Word has carried me through. And not once has He led me on a wrong path."

That's powerful.

> Things don't change when I talk to God; things change when
> God talks to me. When I talk, nothing happens; when God talks,
> the universe comes into existence.
>
> —Bob Sorge

I Hear You

If we were talking over lattes at Starbucks right now, you might tell me how desperately you want to know God's will, how you feel almost in bondage to doubt and uncertainty, how you're afraid to take a step in any direction because you're not sure it's the one He's leading you to take. You want to hear His voice and receive His guidance. And yet from all appearances, it seems as if God is hiding from you—forcing you to hunt and peck, try and guess, hit and miss. And the heaviness of your search and the paralysis of not knowing why He's so silent is weighing you down, stripping you of all joy and confidence.

Well, yes, the Lord expects you to cooperate with Him as He sanctifies your body and soul. He needs you in His Word so you can keep yourself positioned at the junction box, the point where His lines of communication travel the most freely and frequently. That "praying without ceasing" thing, remaining actively aware of His presence throughout the 10:15s and 2:30s of the average day, is crucial to getting your ears open and your heart receptive.

But here's what I want to encourage in you—the big message of this chapter, perhaps the big message of this book. Try never to forget it. Here it is . . .

There's no code for you to crack. No puzzle He's waiting for you to put together. No stick He's dangling in your peripheral vision, then snatching away when you turn your head toward it. He's not sitting up in heaven with the cameras rolling and stopwatches ticking, testing whether or not you're spiritually sharp enough to figure out the next move He wants you to make.

God has taken upon Himself the burden of responsibility for communicating with you.

God has taken upon Himself the burden of responsibility for communicating with you. That's why He made sure His Word was alive. And that's why at the appropriate time, when you're listening, when you're patient, when you're trusting, His voice will resonate with power, punch, and authority.

I can assure you—from the evidence of Scripture, from the centuries of accounts of men and women who have followed Him, from even the limited experience of my own life—He will speak. And you will know. When the Bible talks about us having freedom in Christ, this is at least part of that glorious privilege and spiritual abundance we're allowed to walk in by God's grace. There's no need for you to be burdened by or gripped with a paralyzing fear that you are not in God's will. If you are seeking Him and being obedient to what He has placed before you today, then *you are* in His purposes for now, and that is all He is asking of you and of me.

That's why I no longer go around frantically searching for God's will. I just diligently search for God. I trust from His Word that it is His responsibility to show me what He wants me to do and how I'm supposed to go about doing it—that if I focus on keeping my spiritual ears open, I will hear His voice when He speaks.

You'll hear Him too.

He'll speak persistently. He'll speak personally. He'll speak with peace. He'll speak with challenge. And He'll roll it all together in the eternal counsel of His truth until His message echoes in your heart with heaven-sent authority.

That's the voice of God.

Chapter Challenges

- Expect God's voice to resonate with an authority and weight that other influences do not have.

- Realize that Scripture is not just the boundary into which everything God says will fall but is itself the chief means through which He will speak.

- Watch for the Spirit to personalize Scripture, making it connect with your current circumstances.

- The responsibility for our knowing God's will falls primarily on Him. Do not be burdened by fear of failure or paralyzed by "not knowing." At the right time, He will reveal His will.

- If you are being obedient regarding the responsibilities He has placed before you today, you are in His will for your life.

Part Three

REMEMBER WHAT HE WANTS TO ACCOMPLISH

THE BETTER TO KNOW HIM *Chapter Eleven*

I will give them a heart to know
Me, that I am the Lord.

Jeremiah 24:7 NIV

A person never really exhausts the question, "What does God's voice sound like?" You could work your way down every column on *Jeopardy!*, complete the most successful run in game show history, and still only dip one toe in the water. God has told us much in His Word and by His Spirit, but truly heaven alone will unlock the breadth and scope of what hearing from Him is all about.

In the last section we've explored *how* He speaks, but He is far too vast and amazing to be captured by a few chapters. Even a few million.

We can get hung up on the mechanics of how He speaks; but I believe that one of the "secrets" of hearing His voice is simply found in recognizing *why* He would speak: What are His goals? What does He desire to accomplish? The answers to these questions are diametrically opposed to the Enemy's. So the more clear we are on "why," the more clearly we can separate God's voice from others.

One of the principal answers to this question is discovered by considering the goals that have been on the heart of God from the beginning of time. Woven through the Bible—from Old Testament to New—is His desire to have friendship with His people, one in which He is not only known but experienced in some capacity. In the Old Testament, there was a barrier between Yahweh and His followers, since the high priest alone had access to Him once a year on the Day of Atonement—the most important day on the religious calendar of Israel—when sacrifices would be offered to atone for the people's sin. And yet even during this time, Yahweh still made Himself known to the likes of regular people like Gideon and Samuel, and responded to Hannah's prayer. When Jesus was crucified, that temple veil was literally torn, symbolizing the unparalleled access that all people could have with God. The barrier is gone.

He has even gone so far as to put His Spirit within those who believe so that we can know Him in more personal ways than ever before.

This means that anything we hear from God will be designed to glorify Him and reveal His very nature to us. Absolutely nothing we hear from God through the Holy Spirit will contradict His nature or His Word or seek to detract from our intimacy with Him. His personal word to us will inevitably reveal who He is.

Our Enemy, on the other hand—the father of lies—will seek to deceive us in any way he can. When he speaks to us, we'll know *his* voice because he will distort the character and Word of God. Anything you hear that doesn't magnify and highlight the character of God is not a message from Him.

God's desire is not merely for us to receive information that applies to our lives but to recognize more about who He is.

When God speaks and causes your spiritual ears to hear Him, it is for the purpose of making Himself known to you. And not just in a textbook way. He wants to turn your knowledge of Him into your experience of Him. So when He speaks, you'll recognize His voice because in following its directive, you will be put into position to experience God's character in your life.

The Enemy, or your ego, or even your very own mind will often lead you down the path that shields you by keeping you comfortable. The voice of God, however, will reveal an attribute of Himself that is available for you to experience. He'll encourage you to take *that* route—the one that will most clearly cause you to discover and personally experience an attribute of God.

The Spirit's primary goal is to bring glory to the Father (John 16:14), so His message to you will accomplish this objective on some level, causing you to see the Lord exalted and leading you into a more intimate relationship with Him. So He will maneuver you into places where you can experience Him in new, deeper ways.

Take Nancy and Jeff. When Hurricane Katrina struck, the high wind and floodwaters completely destroyed their Louisiana home, sparing their lives but not their property and possessions. Like many, they wondered what to do next, how they were (literally) going to pick up the pieces and put their lives back together.

And yet they couldn't shake the fact that both of them were hearing a challenging message from God to ignore their limited resources and begin reaching out to the families around them who had lost loved ones in the storm. No, it didn't sound rational. Didn't logically follow the deep sense of personal loss and distress they were experiencing. But God was persistent as they sought Him through prayer and Scripture. They realized that if they wanted to know Him in a whole new way, this was the place to do it. Right here. Without a roof over their head or a spare dollar in their dwindling savings account.

While personally ministering to dozens of devastated families during those difficult months and years following Katrina's fury, God miraculously supplied them with free housing and job opportunities that replenished their once weakened financial position. They became His hands and feet on the ground in a historic disaster zone by helping those in need in very practical ways, and He became the guardian and provider they might never have experienced if they had resisted His voice and concentrated all their energies on alleviating their own problems. He became for them *Jehovah-Rohi*—"God our shepherd."

They didn't just know it now because they'd read it in the Bible. They *knew* it through their own experience.

When God speaks, His desire is not merely for us to receive information that applies to our lives but to recognize more about who He is. Even salvation itself, which obviously comes with a heavenly benefit package and tons of valuable perks, is really all about one thing—knowing God. "This is eternal life," Jesus once said while praying to His Father, "that they may know You, the only true God, and Jesus Christ whom You have sent" (John 17:3). In the original language, the word "know" is *ginosko*, which relates to familiarity acquired through experience—the kind of knowledge Jesus Himself prayed that we would possess, one that results in an experience of who He is.

He doesn't just want you to *hear* Him. He wants you to *experience* Him—to experience Him so you can *know* Him.

That's why He speaks—to reveal more about Himself to you, to move your relationship with Him from an academic one to an experiential one as you hear His instruction and respond in obedience.

Therefore, knowing Him and relating personally with Him is not only something you do that enables you to hear His voice better (as we've talked about before). When God places you in a challenging situation, take it as a signal that He will be glorified—and that you will come to know Him in a deeper way. Because He's going into the challenge with you.

And you'll know Him even better on the other side.

A little knowledge of God is worth more than a great deal of knowledge about Him.

—J. I. Packer

More Than a Name

In Scripture, people's names often stand for something specific about their character or their story. When God gave Hannah a baby after years of her fervent praying, "she named him Samuel, saying, 'Because I have asked him of the Lord'" (1 Samuel 1:20). David, the "man after [God's] own heart" (1 Samuel 13:14), is a Hebrew name meaning "beloved." The earthly name given to the incarnate Son of God—Jesus—means "Yahweh is salvation."

Similarly, the Bible uses many names for God to help us know specific things about Him. Different circumstances elicit different names that describe His character. Jerry and I have seen God amaze us with His unexpected financial blessing and favor, so we have experienced Him as *Jehovah-Jireh*—"God our provider." He revealed Himself as *El-Shaddai*—"the all-sufficient God." We'd known this before through the pages of Scripture and through the testimony of others, but now we knew it ourselves.

Another of our friends—I'll call her Marcia—is experiencing God in a circumstance that seems about as hopeless as it possibly could. If ever there were an innocent party in a divorce proceeding, she would qualify as one. Her husband, the last person in the world you'd anticipate being unfaithful to his wife, has followed one of Satan's favorite, most predictable lies—the illusion of adulterous satisfaction. And still remaining heavily influenced by this deception, he has declared his intentions to divorce. The dissolution of their marriage is well under way. Marcia, of course, has ample biblical grounds to see it end, and she admits having days when she looks forward to being free of it all.

But not today. Lately, as she pours out her heart to God and listens for His response, He's been leading her to do something she's not really interested in doing. He's confirming that His will for her during this heart-wrenching season of life is to keep praying for her husband, believing for his return to their home and family.

This is why He speaks—to cause us to encounter Him in a way that we otherwise might not have the privilege of seeing or being part of.

This is crazy—isn't it? Might be, unless, as she said the other day, "I know if I keep on praying for him, not just wiping my hands of him, I will get to experience God in a way I never have before and may never have an opportunity to do so otherwise." This may or may not work out the way she wishes it would. But either way, she's going to walk forward into life with her hand firmly in the grip of *Jehovah-Nissi*—"the Lord our banner";

El-Berith—"God of the covenant." There's no telling what attributes of God she'll come to know by obeying His leading in this area.

The Enemy would never ask you to do such a thing—would never require you to trust God more fully, to rely on Him so desperately and completely. He would never want you to know God at levels of nearness and intimacy that can often only occur in the most difficult set of circumstances. He won't direct you into a situation where you'll experience God manifesting Himself more peacefully and powerfully than ever. Your knowing God better through challenging circumstances isn't, of course, part of the Enemy's plan. In fact, by responding with obedience and greater intimacy with God, you're actually thwarting Satan's purposes.

So what will God do to bring us closer to Him? He'll tell Noah to build an ark to keep him and his family safe in the "rain." He'll tell Abraham to sacrifice his beloved son Isaac. He'll tell Gideon that deliverance will come with a mere three hundred soldiers. He'll tell the disciples to throw their nets to the other side of the boat when they've already been fishing without success all night.

This is why He speaks—to cause us to encounter Him in a way that we otherwise might not have the privilege of seeing or being part of.

> When He, the Spirit of truth, comes, He will guide
> you into all the truth; for He will not speak on
> His own initiative, but whatever He hears,
> He will speak; and He will disclose to you what
> is to come. He will glorify Me, for He will take
> of Mine and will disclose it to you.
> John 16:13–14

Whatever Helps Me Know You

The familiar story of the Old Testament character Job is most often noted for the extreme suffering and hardship he endured, seemingly without reason. And yet if you can pull yourself back from the accounts and descriptions of his various trials—out where the view is a little more wide-angle and panoramic—you see that his losses and afflictions are not the main story here. One of God's reasons for allowing these happenings in Job's life was not to hurt him or punish him, but to enable this man to *know* Him.

This reality comes to a dramatic head near the end of the book, where after enduring such an intense season of difficulty, and putting up with some questionable counsel from friends, Job's heart was finally primed to hear some things he might not have been ready to receive before, even though he was described as a "blameless, upright" man (Job 1:1).

So that's when God spoke up—to make Himself known.

Against the backdrop of Job's difficult circumstances, God painted a portrait of Himself so that Job could see Him as He is. Through a series of pointed questions, He revealed all the things about Himself that Job needed to know—His power. Righteousness. Omniscience. Sovereignty.

And Job got the message. Having been stripped bare of much that had given his life meaning and satisfaction, he now could say to God, "I had only heard about you before, but now I have seen you with my own eyes" (Job 42:5 NLT).

Job had known *about* God. But now he'd been enabled, by God's words, to *know* Him.

This is precisely what God wants, and He will allow the measures necessary to achieve it. So whether what you're going through right now is confusing, stretching, painful, awkward, tiring, embarrassing, or even wildly exciting—the point of it all is to help you hear God in the midst of it. Even if you are frustrated by what appears to be God's indifference as you sit in seeming silence, waiting for His direction, even the silence can often be God's chosen means to compel you to press into Him in a way you otherwise wouldn't. His silence can create a holy hunger in your heart you might not otherwise have.

> *God's* goal in your life is to move you from a mental knowledge of Him to an experiential one.

So don't be frustrated by what you are experiencing. This journey is worth it—even *this* part of it—if it more fully enables you to experience God.

God's goal in your life—just as in Job's life—is to move you from a mental knowledge of Him to an experiential one. For without experiential knowledge of the nature of God, your obedience becomes more difficult, perhaps even impossible. The more you know and believe to be true about who God is and what He can do, the more willing you become to trust Him, submit to Him, and let Him lead you into His will.

But God is personal, remember? What He requires of one is not necessarily what He requires of another. He knows you intimately—better than you know yourself. He knows *exactly* what you need in order to experience Him most fully and completely, and He can be trusted to direct you by the sound of His voice to those places, circumstances, and events where you are best positioned to walk in true intimacy with this Lover of your soul. So when seeking to discern His leading, ask yourself: *Which option will cause God to be most glorified and enable me to know Him in a way I might not otherwise get to?*

When faced with choices that won't wait for the clarity you are seeking, prayerfully assume He is leading you to take the path in which He will be most glorified and will lead you to the deepest experience with Him. In some cases—yes—it may not mean the easiest way. But by being assured that He is setting you up to know Him better in the process, you can likewise be assured that He will bear you up as you forge ahead with Him.

That's "why" He's leading you this way.

To know Him is the grand goal and adventure of life. Inviting you into more intimate fellowship with Him will always be one of His primary reasons for steering you in one direction or the other.

Don't just be listening to hear Him. Be listening to know Him.

Chapter Challenges

- When discerning God's voice, consider which option will bring Him the most glory and draw you into a more experiential relationship with God.

- Pinpoint and disregard the alternative that detracts from God's character or will keep you from depending on Him more fully.

- God's apparent silence is often His chosen means of communication. Do not be frustrated while waiting. Consider what God may be trying to say to you through the silence.

SOUNDS LIKE A PLAN

Chapter Twelve

We are God's masterpiece. He has created
us anew in Christ Jesus, so we can do the
good things he planned for us long ago.

Ephesians 2:10 NLT

Kimberly is a mother of four. And years ago, she sensed that the Lord was leading her to minister to women. Her ultimate desire was that God would open up opportunities for her to speak to other women in conference settings all over the country.

So you can imagine how disheartened she became when she didn't receive many invitations to do what she really wanted to do with her life, what she thought God had led her to pursue. Even with a nice brochure printed up, even with a targeted mailing list, she wasn't getting the kind of response that enabled her to cut loose and give this her complete attention.

Meanwhile, Kimberly's sixteen-year-old daughter was the social type. And their home was one where her friends always felt welcome to come over and make themselves comfortable. During many of these fun times together, Kimberly found herself engaged with these girls in conversations that often led to spiritual matters.

One day while praying and meditating on the Word, Kimberly realized that even though her desire to travel from city to city as a women's ministry leader hadn't yet come to fruition, God was bringing young women right into her living room who were hungry for intimacy with the Father. He was opening her eyes to see that He had a plan, and was going so far as to bring it right into her own house!

Today, she has a flourishing ministry to women, just as she always thought God had said she would. But instead of following her own plans for herself, she's following God's plans. Each week her front room fills up with teenage girls who hang on her every word as she delivers to them the Word of God. When she accepted His invitation to join Him in His work, He enabled her to experience His power in her activities.

Why does God speak? Not only to bring you into an experience with Him but to allow you to be a part of the experiences that He has prepared long ago. He has plans and wants you to be a part of carrying them out.

Most often He does this by allowing your spiritual eyes to be opened so that you become aware of His activity on earth. When this occurs, this is your invitation to join Him in His kingdom purposes, both for your own life as well as His designs for this generation.

Seeing God's hand is hearing God's voice.

Nothing pleases God more than when we ask for what He wants to give. When we spend time with Him and allow His priorities, passions, and purposes to motivate us, we will ask for the things that are closest to His heart.

—Bruce Wilkinson

His Plan with Your Name on It

When you think about it, the beauty of Jesus' life on earth was not merely that He did His Father's will, but rather that He did His Father's will *and nothing else*. Even as the living Son of God, He still didn't come up with new ideas and strike out on His own. He understood a principle we often forget: True success in any endeavor can only come when the Father has initiated the activity and invited our participation. And one reason He could so fully engage in the activities given to Him by His Father is that He hadn't expended all of His time, energy, and effort in peripheral undertakings.

Even before you and I were born, God had an agenda for our careers, our finances, our families, our everything. He has always known what He wants to do with us. We are often so overwhelmed and bogged down by activities that *are not* a part of His plans, we don't have any drive left to participate in the ones that *are* His for us to fulfill. And we as His children are the most blessed, the most fulfilled, and the most effective when we're engaged with the things He put us on this earth to do. His plans take preference over ours.

And He invites us to participate in them.

When He speaks, this is a big reason why.

How many times have you invited yourself to do something—to start it when you want to start it, to end it when you want to end it, to see it how you want to see it? I can't even begin to tell you how often I've plowed ahead with my own plans rather than waiting for God's invitation. No wonder so many of them have fallen flat. They weren't His; they were mine.

But when your continual prayer is, "Lord, open my eyes to see where you are working," the indwelling Holy Spirit will allow you to see God's movement and discern His inviting voice so you can see His work and respond to His leading to get involved. Again, remember that Jesus promised, "Anyone who wants to do the will of God will know" whether it's His voice doing the leading or something else (John 7:17 NLT).

> *Ask* God to keep you spiritually alert in every single season of your life, so you can see His movements and be aware of His activity.

So we must not only consider whether we'll be able to *hear* it, but also if we will *accept* it. Will we give up our own plans and follow His? Will we leave room for Him to ask us to do something that's different than we had anticipated?

When my pastor looked at me across the table in a meeting one day and said, "Priscilla, I want you to coordinate the women's conference at church," I was excited.

I knew that this ministry needed revitalizing. So I was thrilled that God would allow me to try restarting the engine of the hearts of the women in our fellowship through a conference that included worship and Bible teaching.

I appointed a committee and we started making plans. But as word of our reformatted conference started getting out into the community, we not only began receiving acceptance among our church family but also interest from many other women's ministries, even from other cities and states. My initial reaction was to remain focused on my plan to make the conference just for the women of our church, but the calls kept coming. More and more it was becoming apparent that women outside our church needed this conference too.

For six months it went on like this. The phone calls, the inquiries . . . the interest caught our committee by surprise. We weren't set up to handle an influx of visitors. Yet even as the date neared—close enough that some of our final decisions were already being implemented—we went back to God in prayer to seek His will, to see if He indeed wanted us to enlarge our vision and scope for this new event.

Did He ever.

Today, when The "Desperate for Jesus" women's conference rolls around each summer, thousands of women gather from nearly every Christian denomination to spend a couple of days together in the presence of the Lord. Now under the leadership of another, the unifying work of this ministry continues to astound me. It is God's work. No doubt about it.

If our committee had ignored His plans while stubbornly or short-sightedly pursuing our own, our church might have missed a great opportunity to minister to women nationwide—even worldwide—and to unite sisters across breaches that would normally divide them. Many of the friendships and mentoring relationships that have blossomed from this unique spiritual experience might never have developed, at least not in the exact way God has chosen to connect women from all different walks of life and all different areas of the country.

It's been truly amazing.

But perhaps not as amazing as this: Before our steering committee had scribbled down the first of our big ideas on a legal pad for "our" event—

before any of us were even *born*, in fact—God had already established a desig-nated plan and purpose for this conference. The question He was asking me was, "Would I join in with His purposes, or would I rigidly keep my head down and pursue my own?" Certainly no one is capable of standing in the way of God's kingdom agenda, but if we had been unwilling to listen for His voice and submit to His direction, we easily could've missed being part of it.

When you see evidence that God is moving in circumstances, and when those circumstances begin leading you down a specific path, you have your cue to join Him. When the "five Ms" begin aligning themselves into an easily-read invitation—the "message" of the Spirit, the "model" of Scripture, the "mode" of prayer, the "ministry" of mature believers, the "mercy" of con-firmation—you should consider yourself part of something only God could dream up and put together. Something He did before you were even born.

His amazing plans for you.

When a young Saul lost track of his donkey in the Old Testament, he had no idea that this inconvenience would lead him to the prophet who was to anoint him king over Israel. While the apostle Paul was locked away in prison, he couldn't have known that this season of incarceration would become the catalyst that produced a number of divinely inspired letters to the first-century churches we're still reading today. When Ruth was left widowed and childless, she had no idea that her story would be central to the coming of the Messiah.

God had a plan—much bigger than the ones any of these people could imagine. And God still has a plan—much bigger than anything you could have arranged, even if your life had gone precisely as you'd always hoped it would.

So don't spend your time wishing yourself out of whatever situation God has placed you in. Instead of craving marriage rather than singleness, instead of desiring to be "upper" rather than "under" class, instead of want-ing a "better" church than the one you already worship with, ask God to open your eyes to the plans of His that are already right here and—even better—close to His heart.

Ask God to keep you spiritually alert in every single season of your life, so you can see His movements and be aware of His activity. Then remain willing to go where He leads, because in doing so, you are responding to the voice of God.

What might He show you if you were willing to do whatever He wanted?

> If anyone serves Me, he must follow Me;
> and where I am, there My servant will be also.
> John 12:26

Perfect Timing

I hope you're starting to feel a surge of confidence, knowing that God is inviting you to join Him in His predestined plans for your life. As you put into practice all the lessons we've learned together along the way about hearing His voice, you'll realize He's not just leading you in any old direction but is involving you in His kingdom agenda for this particular time in history.

That's right. His agenda for this age—the generation in which you are living.

This means that the purposes of God not only involve specific plans; they also involve specific timing. He has not only orchestrated the events in your life but also the chronological framework in which they will occur. When He speaks and allows you to catch sight of His movements, it will be in concert with His perfect sense of timing.

Which sometimes, honestly, will not jibe with yours.

Wonder how many years Elizabeth and Zachariah disagreed with God's timing on providing them a child. They never stopped praying until the days had obviously passed for them to conceive and bear children. Yet one day in the midst of his priestly duties, Zachariah saw an angel beside the altar of incense who said to him, "Your petition has been heard, and your wife Elizabeth will bear you a son," one who "will turn many of the sons of Israel back to the Lord their God. It is he who will go as a forerunner before Him in the spirit and power of Elijah . . . to make ready a people prepared for the Lord" (Luke 1:13, 16–17).

God's plan had not merely been for them to have a child but to have *this* child, this child with a special mission, this child who would come along at this particular moment in history to herald the appearance of Messiah. Elizabeth wasn't too old to be a mother. And God hadn't spoken too late. He had waited until everything was in place for the birth of His Son, and then He gave clear, powerful instructions to those involved.

Perfect timing.

Jeremiah, as we've seen, was called by God to be a prophet to the nations while he was very young. And he was sure the Lord had spoken too soon. He knew he was not yet ready to fill such large spiritual shoes. But God's calling of Jeremiah at that moment was pertinent to God's agenda. It was 627 BC, the thirteenth year of King Josiah's reign in Judah. Many sinful, immoral kings had led the people during the years leading up to this time, men who had no respect for the things of God. But with the emergence of young Josiah on the scene, things were chang-

He'll make His plans clear to you right on time, even as He keeps you loved and encouraged by His presence all along the way.

ing. Second Kings 23 records the wholesale reforms he had instituted, summoning the national leaders to the temple to burn their idols and call out again on the name of the Lord. Josiah was set on transforming the religious landscape of his people. He was calling them back to God.

And God wanted a man just like Jeremiah to declare the Word of the Lord in this kind of cultural climate, a person He had consecrated "in the womb" for such an assignment as this (Jeremiah 1:5). Jeremiah wasn't too young for this job. And God hadn't spoken too soon. He had made His plans known to Jeremiah precisely as the season arrived for the people of God to be more prepared for his prophetic ministry.

Perfect timing.

But, boy, it hasn't always seemed like God was operating with perfect timing in my own life. I've sulked and fumed more times than I can remember when I've needed clarity about a specific circumstance yet felt as though He wasn't providing it. Over and over again, however, He's shown me that the reason He chose to wait was that I would've most assuredly snatched the news from His hand and rushed on ahead of Him.

I know that if He had spoken to me ten years earlier about the details of this ministry He's entrusted to me now, I would either have run impatiently toward it, or run as fast as I could away from it. I was neither spiritually nor emotionally equipped to handle the demands of this work—His work—until the exact moment when He made His will plain.

Perfect timing.

Jesus expressed this idea to His disciples when He said, "I have many more things to say to you, but you cannot bear them now" (John 16:12). In other words, there's a time for everything in your life. God alone knows what that is. And because His Spirit dwells within you, and because He is deeply interested in helping you experience the fullness of His plans for your life, you can just stay tuned and know that He'll make it clear to you right on time, even as He keeps you loved and encouraged by His presence all along the way.

The things that are "freely given to us by God" (1 Corinthians 2:12) are the only things we need to know *now*. A lot of the reason we grow so upset and disturbed about not hearing specifically from God is that we want what isn't "freely given." When we pray, "Lord, show me Your will," we're often asking for things that He knows are not pertinent for another twenty years. We want God to paint the whole picture right away, but He wisely withholds certain truths and information from us until we need it, when we can actually do something with it besides just mess it up.

The Father will wisely show you just what you need to know in order to participate with Him in His plan and program for this season on His calendar. And when He does, get this: the *timing* of His message will be as important as the message itself.

Have confidence in this: if you don't know yet, you don't need to move forward yet.

There is an appointed time for everything.
And there is a time for every event under heaven.
Ecclesiastes 3:1

Now

A decade ago we traveled to the Holy Land, with the goal to see and learn as much biblical history as possible. Thankfully, we had a terrific Jewish scholar as a tour guide who gave us amazing insights at each location. But I remember being so grateful that he didn't just download all that information on us at one time and then leave us alone to our own devices. If he'd done that, there's no way we would have been able to retain what we needed in order to enjoy every location we visited. All along the way, at site after site, he delivered to us what we needed to know as we came to the places where that information was most helpful and valuable. He was the ideal guide.

John 16:13 paints the picture of the Holy Spirit as a "guide," one who gives continuous direction on a need-to-know basis. "He will *guide* you into all the truth." Much of the heartache and frustration I have encountered in discerning God's voice has come from wanting direction from Him before He's been ready to give it. Aren't most of us like these people of Isaiah's day? "Let Him make speed, let Him hasten His work, that we may see it; and let the purpose of the Holy One of Israel draw near and come to pass, that we may know it" (Isaiah 5:19).

But the Holy Spirit doesn't give us all His directions upfront and then leave us alone to sort everything out. Rather, He can be trusted to tell us everything we need to know *for now*, and then to continually update His instructions as we step out in faith and obedience.

We ought to see this as a great blessing, not a begrudging holdout.

So be confident that when it's time for you to know what you need to know, *you will*. If you haven't heard from God on a particular issue, it's not because He's lost your number and doesn't know how to reach you. It may just be because the time is not yet right for Him to clarify this for you.

Bottom line, you have everything you need from Him at this moment. Otherwise, He'd have already given you more. So until God makes His next message clear to you—at the exact right moment, in His perfect knowledge and timing—here's what you should do: *whatever He's told you to be doing right now.* Doing this assures you that you are in God's will for your life.

God is the God of "right now." He doesn't want you sitting around regretting yesterday. Nor does He want you wringing your hands and worrying about the future. He wants you focusing on what He is saying to you and putting in front of you . . . right now.

The voice of the Enemy, by contrast, will often focus on the *past*. What you did. What you didn't do. What you've wasted. What's the use? He'll also focus on the *future*. What could happen. What might go wrong. What others will say. What am I supposed to do next? What makes you think you can do that?

God's voice tells you what you can do *now*, not "if only."

That dear, wise mentor and counselor of so many, Elisabeth Elliot, has said, "One of the best pieces of advice I ever got was, 'Do the next thing.'" Instead of getting all hung up on looking for the grand scope of God's will for your life, just do what He's called you to do right now. That's all that really matters.

Now.

> He said to them, "Follow Me, and I will make
> you fishers of men." Immediately they
> left their nets and followed Him.
> Matthew 4:19–20

Why the Rush?

Here's the blessed fallout of living by this "right now" perspective: If you truly believe that God will speak to you in the appropriate time and place, you should never feel hurried or pressured about making a decision. If you're not clear about something, stay put. Don't move. Only when God has spoken will you be cued to respond in obedience.

Till then? The next thing. The now thing.

That's all you need to do or think about.

Interestingly, some people talk about how Christians don't take their relationship with God seriously enough, don't seem to make the connection between their Sunday worship and their Monday plans. Obviously there's a lot of truth to that. But I'd also say that many Christians—and I'm talking about the active, diligent ones—go too far the other way. They stay all tense and bottled up, nervously seeking God's will, looking high and low for spiritual specifics, then growing dismayed when they can't find them. Even with a clear conscience to guide them, they're sure they must be secretly, subtly failing God, or else He'd be more forthcoming.

Nothing catches God off-guard or alters His agenda.

I want you, dear saint, to leave this chapter trusting Him—His plan and His timing. Breathe deeply with the knowledge that His purposes have been specifically calculated with you and His larger designs in mind, and allow yourself the freedom to sit back and wait, listening for His next message to come whenever He knows the time is right. You haven't necessarily done anything wrong, and you shouldn't necessarily be doing anything more. Just commit to do the "now" thing with faithful simplicity, having full confidence that this *is* the will of God for your life today.

Nothing catches God off-guard or alters His agenda. So when you feel rushed and hurried to make a decision, God is probably not the one speaking. Nowhere in Scripture does He tell anyone to rush into a decision. The Shepherd leads; He doesn't drive. He doesn't force and coerce on the basis of fear and intimidation, not like the Enemy does, frantically working us up into a hurried, unsteady fervor. Instead, God gently encourages and woos. He patiently and persistently gives us enough clarity before requiring our obedience.

If you do not feel assurance in a decision you need to make, then back off. Wait up. Stop and listen for the voice of the Spirit to guide you. Because His voice is always *timely*. He's not behind schedule. As you wait for Him to speak and to fulfill His word to you, stand firm in your faith, trust Him to guide you one step at a time, and then follow wherever He leads.

Let me reiterate: on the occasions when you are pressed for time and a decision has to be made "by noon tomorrow," choose the option that, to the best of your knowledge, will give God the most glory and cause your relationship with Him to flourish.

Our lives, really, are like a box containing all the pieces of a giant jigsaw puzzle. And only God can see the picture on the lid. He alone has a full grasp of the entire layout and knows exactly how (and when) all the pieces need to come together—the arrival of financial assistance, the emergence of a ministry opportunity, the opening of a career promotion or change of direction.

Can you just live with that? Live worry-free? Live watchful, but waiting?

His eternal plans and His perfect timing are gifts to us that enable us to rest in Him and enjoy the adventure of following Him. They free us from the burden of trying to make things happen on our own, from working overtime to make sure everything lines up and comes together at the right time.

It's His job to speak; ours is to listen.

And our joy to be invited to join in.

Chapter Challenges

- Rest in the knowledge that God has a plan for your current circumstances that were prepared before you were born.

- Keep your spiritual eyes open to see where God is already working. This is key for knowing His will for your life. When you catch sight of what He is already doing, this is your cue to get involved.

- God is never hurried, rushed, or behind schedule. If you do not know yet, it's because you don't need to do it yet.

- Zero in on what you know for sure you're supposed to be doing right now, and get busy doing it.

- To make a time-sensitive decision, prayerfully consider which option will bring God the most glory and will encourage a more intimate relationship with Him.

YES, LORD *Chapter Thirteen*

His mother said to the servants,
"Whatever He says to you, do it."

John 2:5

*G*od does not speak just to be heard.

He speaks to be obeyed.

If you take away only a few nuggets of truth from the time we've spent together in these pages, let this be among the most trusted and treasured of them all. Obedience is the alpha and omega of discerning God's voice.

He speaks; we obey.

It's not that easy. But it *is* that simple.

And committing to do so is guaranteed to create a favorable outcome for us and for the Lord's glory.

Monica's life is certainly a case in point. Her friends are blessed and inspired just by hanging around her. Being with her, talking with her, always whets my appetite for a more dynamic relationship with the Lord. She helps me hunger to experience Him personally and powerfully in my everyday existence. I hope you have a friend like that. I hope you *are* a friend like that.

I can think of numerous times when God has shown up so obviously and stunningly that it's almost been too awesome to believe. Like the time when, as her husband struggled to find a new job, their home was saved from foreclosure at the last hour—not once, not twice, but three times (the third time being a random, rare, and simple clerical error that was enough to give them another sixty-day extension). Or the time when the educational needs of their dyslexic son required that he attend a school that specialized in meeting his needs. The prestigious learning center gave him a full scholarship for no reason they could put a finger on.

You want more? She's got more.

And while every account is unique, each one is woven together by a similar theme. A consistent thread. She and I have often talked about this—why some believers like her seem to experience God's supernatural power more often than others, while many Christians can live their entire lives without really witnessing God's handiwork. Her soft, humble answer is this: "I think the reason I see God's activity so clearly in my life is because I've decided that the only appropriate response to Him is complete obedience. I am committed to obeying His leading, no matter how illogical His instructions may seem to be. From giving when I didn't have enough, to making an effort when I was completely out of strength, I've just chosen to do what He says."

He speaks; she obeys.

And then God responds to that obedience—sometimes in ways that are stunning, other times with just a simple yet satisfying holy nod of approval, graced with a deep awareness of His favor, His peace, and His sweet fellowship near.

When God speaks to you, He is asking you to make a commitment. Not just to be *willing* to obey, but to actually follow through. Actually obeying His voice lays the groundwork for Him to continue making His will known to you—not because He relishes playing the role of controlling father-figure, coldly demanding your compliance—but because He desires to bless you with His most special gifts, including deeper intimacy with Him. He knows what is best for you, and He only requires that you obey in order to experience it.

Easy? No.

Simple? Yes.

So will you continue to think of obedience as too high a price to pay, too hard a challenge, too big a risk? Or will you, like Monica, come to the conclusion that it's really the only appropriate response?

> His leading is only for those who are already committed to do as He may choose. To such it may be said: "God is able to speak loud enough to make a willing soul hear."
>
> —Lewis Sperry Chafer

Without Question

How often would you say that you ask for God's opinion while knowing full well you plan to stick with your own? Be honest with yourself. Have you already decided what you're going to do, no matter what you sense His Spirit saying?

I've been known, for example, to ask my husband which pair of shoes he thinks looks best with a particular outfit, though I've already decided which ones to wear. Pull this little bait-and-switch on Jerry enough times, and I can already hear him say, "Why are you asking me? You'll do what you want to do anyway."

This is one of the main reasons hearing God can become so difficult for us—so cloudy, so confusing—is that God, who knows our hearts, doesn't do much speaking into a person's life who isn't dedicated to obeying Him. And once we've begun to choose disobedience over obedience as a pattern, we become increasingly desensitized, our conscience progressively deadened and unable to detect His stirrings. So even when He is speaking, the hardened and dulled heart of the rebellious doesn't sense His holy prodding or pick up His cues from the Scripture. They easily discard any conviction from Him and misinterpret His written Word in order to justify their chosen course of action. As the Scripture says, "Remember, it is sin to know what you ought to do and then not do it" (James 4:17 NLT). Yes, *sin*. The outcome of this? We forfeit intimacy in our fellowship with God and full access to His power operating within and through us.

This is not to say that God is asking or expecting you to be perfect in order to have the privilege of His direction. By no means am I suggesting that you have to *earn* the right to hear God's voice. But the Lord knows how deeply you desire to respond. He knows when your intentions are pure. And what does He promise to the "pure in heart"? Jesus declared it in no uncertain terms: "They shall *see* God" (Matthew 5:8).

He is attracted to those who desire to obey Him and are willing to do so completely.

For example, God didn't call Abraham His "friend" (James 2:23) simply because they enjoyed talking with each other but because Abraham was committed to obeying God's voice regardless of the difficulty. One of Abraham's most astonishing acts of obedience was when God gave him this bizarre set of instructions: "Take now your son, your only son, whom you love, Isaac, and go to the land of Moriah, and offer him there as a burnt offering on one of the mountains of which I will tell you" (Genesis 22:2).

Abraham must have certainly found God's request mind-boggling, not only because he loved Isaac, but also because God had promised that He would make a great nation out of Isaac's descendants. What God was asking Abraham to do seemed irrational. Worse, it seemed to contradict His own word. Abraham didn't understand. Yet he chose to obey anyway, and as a result he saw God's supernatural activity in

Scripture makes clear, over and over again, that the prerequisite for experiencing God is obeying Him.

his life—the angel from heaven, the ram in the thicket, and a new name for that holy location: "The Lord Will Provide" (verse 14).

First, obedience.

Then, the amazing.

I want to see the amazing—God's supernatural activity—and to sense the peace and clear conscience that come from His soothing approbation. I don't want to just hear about it in Abraham's life, in Moses' life, in Monica's life, or even in my beloved parents' lives. I don't want to merely stand off and see it from afar, on the periphery, out on the far fringes of my spiritual potential. I want to *experience* it in a real, tangible way.

The key to opening this door, which seems to be elusive to so many, is the well-worn practice of obedience. The Scripture makes clear, over and over again, that the prerequisite for experiencing God is obeying Him.

Obedience. It's what our Father longs for from His children.

The Lord used a simple experience in my family to demonstrate the power of obedience to me. One of my sons had gone to bed coughing and sneezing. We'd given him some medicine, but it was hardly touching his symptoms. Every few minutes, it seemed, I was being snatched awake to the sound of his struggles upstairs as he tried to sleep. I'd gone up to check on him several times and kept coming back to bed. All night long.

Finally, around 4 a.m., I was awakened not so much by Jerry Jr.'s coughing as by the Spirit of God, who was encouraging me to get up, walk upstairs, lay hands on my son, and pray for his healing. It was a deep-rooted prompting that I knew was from the Lord.

For ten minutes or more I debated with God on the wisdom of this strategy. Didn't He know it was 4 a.m. down here? I was so tired. I'd already been up numerous times, and I'd just gotten warm and settled again, trying to squeeze a full night's sleep into these last couple of hours of darkness. Couldn't I just let my son try to get whatever rest he could, and then deal with this again in the morning?

But I knew where these instructions were coming from. And even in my groggy condition, I wondered if perhaps God's supernatural activity was indeed awaiting my simple obedience. So even though most of me was resistant to follow, my feet finally hit the floor and I was soon back in my son's room, leaning quietly over his bed.

I placed my hands on his head and his back as he lay there, still sniffling and wheezing in an exhausted attempt at sleep. I prayed for God's healing in his little body. I spoke words of Scripture over him. I claimed the promises of God for his life and for this situation, and asked that according to the Lord's will, he would heal. Then after these few whispered moments, I padded back downstairs, curled back under the covers, heard one final cough from his room, and then . . . nothing. He slept soundly the rest of the night and woke the next morning with no sign of illness.

Your instructions from the Lord may be very different than mine were. The point is to be willing to obey whatever He tells you.

This would probably be pinpointed as no more than a mere fluke for some people. But since God had been dealing with me on this very issue in my walk with Him, I knew it was the Spirit's wake-up call to get busy responding to Him immediately, no matter how ill-timed or inconvenient I thought His instructions were.

Upon seeing our son in the morning—bags no longer under his eyes, nose no longer red and swollen from sniffling, and his appetite back to its normal capacity—my husband said to me, "I heard you get up with him around four o'clock. Did you give him some more medicine? I didn't hear him coughing anymore after you went up there."

All I could do was smirk. Yup, I'd given him something, all right.

And I'd been given something as well—another incredible experience with the Lord through which He provided just a tiny glimpse of the potential blessing reserved for those who build a foundation of obedience.

Wonder what supernatural rewards are awaiting each of us if we will just commit to responding to Him in obedience in every situation?

> The worst thing you can do—the quickest way to become insensitive—is to ignore an impression. You must not allow yourself to hear without responding.
>
> —Peter Lord

Without Escape

Choosing to *obey* isn't the only issue we've got to discuss together. The *kind* of obedience we offer is another important aspect to consider. Obedience to God—the kind that invites His continued speaking to us—must be *complete* obedience. Obedience without question or reservation. Obedience that does what He says even over the objections of reason and comfort. Obedience with no hedging or fallback plans.

It's like the total commitment expressed by the Beckett family, who felt the call of God to go minister in a Southern California community infested with gangs and drugs, and who placed their spiritual stake in the ground by purchasing cemetery plots for themselves within the city limits, saying with this one bold action, "Unless God tells us differently, we will die serving Him here."

This is the type of obedience God wants from us. To throw ourselves wholeheartedly into doing whatever He has asked. To respond with radical faith and trust. To realize, as Jesus said, that "those who accept my commandments and obey them are the ones who love me." And to those He makes this promise: "I will love them and reveal myself to each of them" (John 14:21 NLT).

The Greek word for "reveal" in this verse means "to exhibit, to appear in person, to declare." While everyone who believes in Christ, of course, is privileged to know the love of God, those who make obedience a habit in their lives can expect to receive an invasion of His manifest presence— those precious, ever-deeper revelations of His power and glory.

On the other hand, believers who always have an escape plan—another option waiting in the wings, a plan B to revert to—are what the Scriptures call "double-minded" (James 1:8). And they can never expect to fully know and experience the power and presence of God. They can never experience the full disclosure of divine activity that is available to those who are all in. They shouldn't even anticipate that they will "receive anything from the Lord" (verse 7), not the least of which is His continued direction and guidance.

So if you aren't hearing from God very clearly or regularly, ask the Lord to reveal whether or not any double-mindedness is the culprit—any sense of holding back, any initial resistance that blocks your full acceptance and obedience of His message to you.

Think back again to Abraham's experience of hearing God's direction to sacrifice his son Isaac. Think about the intense emotional pain that must have accompanied his three-day journey from Beersheba to Mount Moriah—seventy-two long hours to reconsider and change his mind. But Abraham was committed to following through on these difficult instructions from Yahweh.

He hadn't brought along a spare sacrificial animal to substitute for Isaac at the last minute. Hadn't dodged the ominous task of splitting wood and sharpening his knife before setting out. He was committed to obeying God without excuse or escape.

Completely. Unquestionably.

Only one thing could inspire this kind of wholehearted obedience in Abraham: utter confidence that the God who had led him this far was not only good and kind but would also follow through on His promises. He knew that even in this illogical circumstance, Yahweh was working for his ultimate good. He knew it. Otherwise, he could never have gone through with it.

And unless we're sure of these same things, neither can we.

God has often had to remind me, whenever I can tell that my desire to obey is waning, that *He is love* and *He is good*. These are not mere personality traits of God; they are innate to His being. And while that doesn't mean I'll always enjoy His choices, knowing these certainties about Him assures me that He will never ask me to do anything that is not both best for me and in keeping with His plan. If I can just trust that, then I can be sure He will supply me with the strength to accomplish whatever He's sent me to perform—no matter how great, no matter how small.

> The Lord God has opened My ear; and I was not
> disobedient nor did I turn back. . . . Therefore, I have
> set My face like flint, and I know that I will not be ashamed.
> Isaiah 50:5, 7

Without Delay

We've talked before in this book about when it is appropriate to delay an upcoming action or decision until you've heard from the Lord. There's much biblical wisdom and prudence in that perspective. But once you've heard from God, delay is no longer an option—only instant obedience is.

Abraham not only obeyed, but he obeyed without delay. In fact, every time God gave him instructions, he obeyed immediately. Take a look at his track record . . .

- When God told him to leave his homeland, Abraham "went forth" right away (Genesis 12:1, 4).

- When God told him exactly what kind of offering to make, Abraham immediately did exactly what he'd been asked (Genesis 15:9–10).

- When God gave him instructions to circumcise every male in his household, Abraham did it "the very same day" (Genesis 17:23).

- And when God told him to sacrifice his son Isaac, he "rose early " the next morning to accomplish the task (Genesis 22:1–3).

"Early in the morning"?
Huh?

Unlike Abraham, I'm pretty sure I would've waited at least a couple of days before taking the drastic step of sacrificing my son—hoping that just maybe God would change His mind or realize He'd called the wrong person. When the Lord gives me directives that I don't particularly care for or I'm afraid to carry out, the last thing I want to do is get up "early in the morning" to do them. I procrastinate. I think about it. I pray about it. I talk to friends about it. And if I'm not doing any of those, I usually just try to ignore it.

Suffice to say, when instructions from God are difficult—like Abraham's were, like yours and mine often are—we tend to be slow to obey. Yet when God told him to do the unthinkable, Abraham immediately left for the mountain. And because he obeyed at once, he experienced God's divine intervention.

I've sometimes wondered if that ram would've been caught in the bush if Abraham had waited a day, a week, perhaps even a month or more to do what God had told him. I don't know. Only God knows. But what we do know for sure is this: because Abraham immediately obeyed, God's deliverance was waiting on the mountaintop when he arrived.

What would happen if we just ran with *that*?

Is it possible that we'd see God's activity more frequently? Would our experience of Him be more full and rich? Instead of caving to fear about what the possible outcomes might be, could we just believe that our immediate obedience would be met with His supernatural providence that has been prepared ahead of time. Instead of wavering in worry and insecurity, could we just trust that He knows what He's doing and why He's saying this, and that He will give us further details when the time comes for needing them.

Could we just say, "Yes, Lord"?

Then we'd be giving Him what He desires—the only appropriate response. Even if we were still unclear on all the reasons why God commanded this in the first place, we'd be giving Him what He desires—obedience. We'd feel better about ourselves because His Spirit would comfort us and confirm His approval of our actions. And better yet, we'd open the door for Him to do what He really wants with us.

Several years ago, I fully intended to go back to Dallas Theological Seminary to get a doctoral degree. I'd been thinking about it for quite some time and had even gone through the time-consuming admissions process, including writing a number of required essays and soliciting multiple requests for personal letters of recommendation. I spent many hours making sure that all the forms were filled out correctly before I packaged them all up and drove to the school to drop them off. I'll never forget the excitement I felt, knowing that I would soon be back studying in the classroom.

But while I was driving to the seminary to hand in my application, the Holy Spirit spoke clearly to my heart. *"I didn't tell you I wanted you to go back to school,"* He seemed to be saying. *"You came up with this idea all on your own. I have other plans for you."*

Whoa. Wasn't expecting that.

I mean, here I was, on my way to campus, my crisp packet of materials resting in the seat beside me, and now I was being met with an about-face directive from God that was so strong, I had no doubt He was speaking to me.

Caught in the moment, I thought about just going ahead and dropping off the application anyway. After all, I'd come this far and could always call back later and request that they disregard it. Once the stuff was turned in, I'd go home, talk it over with Jerry, and if we came to this same, unexpected conclusion—even at this late date in the process—I'd call and cancel it. No problem. But if, on the other hand, we determined that I was mistaken in what I thought God was saying about changing course, then finishing my errand would save me another trip out here and I wouldn't miss any deadlines.

But even at that precise moment in the passing lane, the Lord brought to mind this very principle of immediate obedience that we've been talking about. With one swift move by the Spirit, this story of Abraham's radical obedience became a seal on the conviction welling up within me. Yup, I was sure what I should do. So I took the next exit off the freeway and went straight back home—completed application and all.

And then . . .

Within weeks, God began weaving a web of events that would lead to the ministry in which my husband and I are now engaged, something that wouldn't have fit well with the workload of doctoral study—something I didn't know, but God did. We also started a family—a bit unexpectedly. And while I know for certain a woman can be a mom and get a doctorate degree, the Lord knows my threshold for commitments.

In all the years since then, I've never once had my desire rekindled to go back to school—at least for that degree. God has completely removed this aspiration, replacing it with a passion for our ministry and our family. I didn't know at the time all that God had planned for me, but *He* knew. Immediate obedience kept me blessed and protected.

But I'll be the first to admit that there are some areas of obedience—some I'm committed to right now—for which I still don't quite see any outcome that causes it to make complete sense. Just in the past month, as I've been working on this manuscript, a few of the paragraphs I've written took me off guard

Is there something He's speaking to you about right now? Some person to forgive? Some habit to forsake?

as their message began to stir deeply within me God's conviction to discontinue my involvement in a particular activity. It's nothing sinful, by any means, but I just couldn't shake the sense that God wanted me to stop.

Within a couple of days, He confirmed it through an offhand comment made by one of my siblings who was completely unaware of my conviction. With this, I just decided to obey, even though in my opinion there was no reason to have to stop participating in this hobby that I enjoyed so much. But I did . . . and I still am. I miss it, but I can live without it. And living with the peace and confirmation of a clear conscience, as well as the joy of the Lord, is worth it.

Is there something He's speaking to you about right now? Some person to forgive? Some habit to forsake? Some purchase to forgo? If you know it's the Lord, and you can't move ahead as planned without a catch in your conscience, you really have no choice if you desire to see God accomplish His best work in your life, your home, your family.

You must obey His voice. Immediately.

> I will hurry, without delay, to obey your commands.
> Psalm 119:60 NLT

Next Stop, the Supernatural

Now I doubt if any of the themes from this chapter have really come as a big surprise. We all know that nothing good ever comes from disobeying God, and that we never really feel good about our excuses for it. But if we're hoping for a steady dose of abundant life, we've got to take this matter seriously.

So I guess all that's really left for any of us to ask ourselves is whether or not we're prepared to do it. Whether or not we're going to obey Him. And if so, how can we know if we're capable of it, that we can actually do it when the time comes?

Bottom line: waiting until you're in the thick of it to make a resolution to get on with it probably won't work. When you're staring into the face of what appears at the time to be an unreasonable task, and you've not already determined that obedience will be your choice, then you'll be in a hard position that's difficult to maneuver and easy to talk yourself out of. Tomorrow's obedience is something you should go ahead and decide on today, before the next challenge arises.

Remember, God speaks to you in order to invite you into His purposes. This often means you will need to abandon what you thought would be the best route to take so you can do what God is asking of you. And if you and I do not prepare ahead of time to modify our plans as necessary, we will end up frustrated and overwhelmed—not the best frame of mind for following Him obediently into any situation.

- Nicodemus had to modify his belief system in order to be saved (John 3).

- The woman at the well modified her behavior and became an evangelist to her whole city (John 4).

- Joshua had to forgo his battle plans to experience victory at Jericho (Joshua 6).

- Jonah had to be willing to leave the comforts of Israel to go to Nineveh and offer God's mercy to His enemies.

It's never just about hearing and listening.

It's always about obeying—which requires a firm resolve backed by the empowerment of God's Spirit.

Jesus offered an invitation to the people of His day, saying, "Come to Me, all who are weary and heavy-laden, and I will give you rest" (Matthew 11:28). All were invited to partake in this eternally comforting blessing of the kingdom of God—on one condition. They had to "come." They had to make a decision to turn away from their current religious beliefs, traditions, and plans in order to receive the Messiah as their Lord and Savior. They could not continue walking down their own paths, unwilling to flex their own plans, and come to Jesus at the same time.

God wants you to experience Him, to learn more about Him.

And every day as believers in Christ, we too must decide to adjust our lives in obedience to God, surrendering our wills to His. We must keep our plans flexible, not hardened in concrete, leaving room for Him to ask us to do something different than what is written in our datebook.

Even Abraham, our biblical model throughout this chapter, had to make adjustments in order to experience God's best. When he thought his son Ishmael would work out just fine as the child of God's promise, seeing as how Abraham and Sarah had been unable (and were now way too old) to have children of their own, God said, "No. Adjust your thinking, Abraham. I am God, and I can do anything."

This willingness and ability to constantly swivel in God's direction would come in handy later when Abraham was blindsided with those divine instructions to sacrifice his son Isaac. But by that time, he had learned from experience everything he needed to know in order to stay in tune with God's plans and to keep following through—without question, without escape, without delay. He knew for sure that immediate and complete obedience was the best and only appropriate response.

And you can have that same confidence too. Start by just resolving to obey God for the next twenty-four hours. Ask Him to make you sensitive to His leading from sunup to sundown today, responding promptly to every single supernatural nudge you experience. As you go throughout the rhythms of your everyday life, commit to responding in obedience, and just see what unfolds. No telling what the Lord might do that encourages and compels you to make this commitment for a lifetime.

God wants you to experience Him, to learn more about Him. He wants to involve you in His purposes, to be part of what He's actively doing on earth, even right in your corner of the world.

And perhaps most importantly, He wants you to obey, to see whatever supernatural thing He wants to do next in your life.

Come on, now, you know you don't want to miss out on that.

Chapter Challenges

• God's people often do not experience His activity because they haven't laid the framework of obedience on which it flourishes. In the next twenty-four hours, commit to obeying whatever you sense God's Spirit compelling you to do, no matter how small or large the task. Record anything significant that happens as a result of your obedience.

- Remember that tomorrow's obedience hinges on today's commitments.

- Don't just determine to obey immediately; also obey completely.

- Recognize that disobedience causes the heart to harden and become desensitized to God's future leading. Don't be deceived into thinking you can hold on to certain areas of resistance to God's will and expect to hear God's voice clearly.

- You can obey without hesitation because God is kind, He is good, and He loves you.

GREATER
EXPECTATIONS *Chapter Fourteen*

Wait and hope for and expect the Lord;
be brave and of good courage and let your
heart be stout and enduring. Yes, wait
for and hope for and expect the Lord.

Psalm 27:14 AMP

$\mathcal{I}$f you were to pick up a copy of the original version of this book, you'd find that the thoughts I shared at the beginning of that manuscript got bumped to the end in this one. Not because I thought they were less important or weren't critical enough to carry the weight of the beginning. On the contrary, I wanted them here purposefully, right at the end of our journey through these pages together, because it's what I wanted to be on your mind and tucked in your heart when you close the cover for the final time.

I wanted for you the same thing that I received—an enthusiastic send-off into the journey of hearing God that left me inspired and full of holy anticipation. I can't ever forget it: a wise mentor facing me head-on with eyes that sparkled with a twinge of holy fervor, placing her hands squarely on my shoulders, and telling me to live in a mode of expectation as I never had before. To look toward each day and every moment in it with the knowledge that God had invaded its space and was eager to communicate with me so that I could join Him in His efforts. To have my eyes and ears perked up and on alert, ready to hear His voice and believe that it would arrive in due time.

I took heed and I haven't regretted it.

Indeed, an expectant heart is a heart ready to hear.

In all honesty, these final thoughts are appropriate in this position now because over the past several years since *Discerning the Voice of God* was originally penned, my expectation of God's activity has only grown. Having a divine expectation and holy anticipation was the beginning of my story then, but now it's the continuation. It's what keeps the adventure fresh and exciting, what makes us want more than when we first began.

It seems that this is a pattern in our relationship with God. The more you hunger, the more He fills. The more He fills, the hungrier you are for Him to keep on filling. It's a constant cycle that keeps you wanting deeper depths and higher heights as the journey continues.

And, unbelievably, He keeps on giving.

So this is a fitting close, I think, designed to relay to you that although the book may be ending, your amazing journey—whether you're a fledging believer or seasoned saint—is just beginning anew today. There's no telling what He's got in store.

So I'm imagining my arm around your shoulder as I send you off with a blessing that I pray you can wake up to every morning—even on days when you're distressed and discouraged right from the start. Even when Satan has pestered you with memories of the past and cruel words of condemnation. Even when for a fleeting moment you begin to feel abandoned by God, as if you've apparently been left off His blessing list.

If discerning the voice of God begins with listening for Him, as we talked about at first, then *continuing* to hear the voice of God is the result of another deliberate choice that—like listening—doesn't depend on what you've done or haven't done for Him, but rather on what *He* has done and still longs to do in you. As you *seek* to hear His voice, do one more thing: *expect* to hear it.

Wake up expecting.

Arrive expecting.

Come expecting.

Live expecting.

Never stop . . .

Expecting.

I have spoken with many Christians from every kind of background and church experience, and it's not hard to deduce from their testimony that they, like many of us—when it gets right down to it—don't really expect God to speak to them and give specific directions concerning the details of their lives. Even if other people can't tell it from the way we walk and talk and carry ourselves in public, lots of us spend the better part of each day doubting that He's going to change anything or at least give us explicit directives concerning our particular set of circumstances. So we wake up, we get ourselves ready, we go through the paces of the day, glad that God is there, of course, but not really expecting much from Him in the way of divine instruction.

But when we truly expect, He incredibly delivers.

> I will stand on my guard post and station myself
> on the rampart; and I will keep watch to see
> what He will speak to me.
> Habakkuk 2:1

What Do You Expect?

Did you catch the title of this section? As I look back over most of my Christian life, my answer would be an emphatically hearty "Not much!" It's true. I anticipated little, and I'm pretty certain that the result of this low level of expectation was an even lower level of experience with God.

He graciously opened my eyes to this on an occasion when I found myself in need of emotional restoration. On the heels of a betrayal that had left me a bit wounded, I searched for a solution. And the Spirit began to convict me that I was seeking help from everyone else but Him. I'd asked for advice from wise counselors and took seriously their recommendations. I'd sought guidance from Internet sites and related books on the subject. I'd done everything I could think of to get an answer to my problem except to lay my request before God. Hadn't even prayed about it.

And as I searched my heart at the Holy Spirit's prompting to see why I hadn't been inclined to go to the Lord with my concern—at least in *addition* to, if not more appropriately *ahead* of, these other sources of aid and information—I quickly discovered two reasons.

First, I didn't truly expect the Lord to speak to me. I didn't anticipate that He would enter my world with a practical, personal, life-changing word.

Second, I didn't expect the Lord to heal me. I knew that the Lord was able to handle my issues, not only through the evidence of His handiwork in Scripture, but also in the lives of many modern-day believers. But in the deepest recesses of my heart, I never really thought He would restore *this.* In *me.*

Then into this revealing moment, with my heart and doubts and attitudes sufficiently exposed, God directed my Bible study into the slender opening of Scripture called the book of Habakkuk, where He used the descriptive message of this prophetic account to teach me an important lesson—a lesson I knew but didn't really *know* until this occasion. With the promises of one simple yet profound verse, the Lord encouraged my pursuit of His word and affirmed His promise to give me counsel.

> For the vision is yet for the appointed time; it hastens
> toward the goal and it will not fail. Though it tarries,
> wait for it; for it will certainly come, it will not delay.
> Habakkuk 2:3

Read those promises again . . . slowly. Digest them. Celebrate them. This is the precise message that God Himself wanted to share with the despondent prophet in the face of trying circumstances and an ever-diminishing pool of holy expectation:

- His message and its fulfillment has "an appointed time."
- The vision "hastens toward the goal."
- God's plans for you "will not fail."

- They will "certainly come" and "will not delay."

Knowing our human proclivity toward discouragement and impatience, God takes a moment to encourage and comfort Habakkuk and, by His Spirit, to do the same for us. For like us, Habakkuk was in need of this reminder.

The prophet was in a state of anguish that had finally gotten the best of him. He had grown increasingly appalled at the sinful nature of the people of Judah and couldn't understand why God wasn't doing anything about it. Habakkuk had prayed and prayed, but God didn't seem to be listening. If He was, He sure wasn't answering.

So when we first meet up with him, this is what we overhear him saying—actually, what we overhear him *praying*:

How long, O Lord, will I call for help, and You will not hear?
I cry out to You, "Violence!" yet You do not save. Why do You
make me see iniquity, and cause me to look on wickedness?
Habakkuk 1:2–3

How long?
And why?
You're probably familiar with the emotions that can trigger those two questions. When the circumstances of life seem to be closing in on you, when you see no end in sight, when you've waited and waited for God to speak into your situation, it's easy to stop expecting much, and you can easily go from waiting to not expecting and then to blaming.

That's apparently what was happening with Habakkuk here. We don't know how long he'd been calling out to God, but we can assume this had been going on for quite a while. Hope had dwindled into discouragement, and all he could see was this rising mountain of sin and rebellion around him—and what was God doing about it? Nothing. Neither to stop it nor to punish it.

Or so it seemed . . .

Look among the nations! Observe! Be astonished! Wonder!
Because I am doing something in your days—you would not
believe if you were told. (verse 5)

Instead of responding thought-for-thought to the prophet's complaint,
God encourages him to look around and see what's already happening.
God tells Habakkuk to stop talking and start looking.

Turns out that while Habakkuk was complaining that God seemed to
be inactive and aloof, God had already been orchestrating a masterful web
of events that were currently in motion. What Habakkuk saw as indolence
was actually God's activity on a whole other level—the kind of activity that
only someone fitted with spiritual vision can ascertain. God was basically
saying, "I *am* speaking, Habakkuk, and I *am* doing something. You've just
been looking through the wrong lens. That's why you can't see it." Rather
than dealing on the same plane with the prophet's narrow, linear way of
viewing things, God showed him that He had a lot more covered than just
his current-day set of issues.

The point that God was trying to make to him—the point He keeps
trying to make to us—is that a heart that continues to anticipate His movement will result in eyes that are open to see and recognize His activity in
the circumstances of life. Indeed, expectation is the root of hearing from
God. If we do not expect God to speak, we will discount the occasions
when He does. We'll assume it was "just a coincidence," or our own idea. We
will not correlate God's work and His Word with the things going on
around us.

But God is *always* working. And if we will keep our eyes open in full
anticipation, we will find that even situations in which He appears to be
indifferent are actually filled with God's handiwork, insight, and instruction
for us.

In Habakkuk's case, God was working behind the scenes, methodically
preparing the Babylonians to be His instrument for disciplining the wayward people of Judah for their sin. Habakkuk's sense of discouragement
was keeping him blinded to this, unable to see God clearly. In *your* case, of
course, it's something else—something He's busy accomplishing beyond

your natural field of vision, out where only He could be doing something so complex and comprehensive that it could occur without your knowledge yet still come to bear on your specific situation.

God is working. Even when it doesn't look like it.

On the authority of God's Word, I can assure you of this.

And knowing this is grounds for your continued expectation. It is the sure foundation on which you can find your footing to keep on eagerly anticipating what He *will do* and is *already doing.*

Even as I write, it occurs to me that this is happening right now in my life in the area of motherhood. I can say with all honesty that my transition to being a parent has taken me by storm—a storm I don't think I was fully prepared to handle. (I guess no mother ever is.) My children are a deep blessing to me—I can hardly contain my love for them in one human heart—but like most moms, there have been days when the weight of this responsibility has brought me to my knees before the Lord. Begging Him to change a certain circumstance or a particular situation we are facing. But as you well know, the rhythm of a mother's day is just that—a rhythm—a staccato cadence of breakfast, lunch, dinner, and dishes in between. So when I saw little changing about the specifics I was praying for, I became discouraged and tended to stop fully believing that God was hearing me, that He would answer me, and that I could ever be the mother He wanted me to be.

Maybe your most pressing burden is something else. A chronic illness. A manipulating parent. A season of unemployment. The specter of bankruptcy. Whatever it is, the thoughts and issues that surround it are continually either on the front burner or in the back of your mind. But God—where is *He?* Conspicuous by His absence? Noted by His silence? Before we know it, our questions begin to sound a lot like Habakkuk's . . .

- "How long, O God, will this circumstance remain the same?"
- "Why, O Lord, aren't You responding to my concerns?"

Let your loving Father's answer to Habakkuk's prayer encourage you, as it's encouraged me. "Look!" See God's hand where you haven't seen it before. Open your eyes to a panorama that stretches far beyond your immediate focus, and witness a God who's doing things in your world and your life that you'd never noticed before.

Because what I'm noticing is what mothers have been experiencing since the beginning of time—God is using my children to produce spiritual fruit in me; something for which I've fervently prayed for years and years but expected to be answered in a much more lofty, much less daily and practical way. When lifelong friends note changes and maturity in me through the years, I've been able to trace it back to my life as a mom—challenges and all—that is pulling out what God wants to be seen in me. Through the unpredictability of their schedule and demands, God is teaching me how to stay flexible to His will, more able to change course and direction, less anchored to my own plans and schedule. Through their dependence on me as their mom, He's teaching me both the cost and the benefits of spiritual fruit like peace, joy, and self-control. Look. Observe. He's working. And He is speaking . . . even when it seems like He is not.

When I was younger, He began allowing me to develop the Spirit's *gifts* in my life. Gave me a good environment and circumstances for doing that. Now He's using this season to develop the Spirit's *fruit* in my life. Noticing this has restored my confidence in the fact that He is speaking and working in my situation, even right now in the midst of the joyful chaos that is motherhood.

It's made me expect even more—in unique, surprising ways I wouldn't have noticed before.

If you have been asking God to change something, and yet you're finding that He appears not to be choosing to, most likely the change He wants to generate is in *you.* Ask Him to open your eyes to see what He is doing and how He is moving.

Because He is.

He's doing it.

And what He is doing *is* His word to you for right now. The more you see, the more you can believe, the more you can hope, the more you can expect.

Those who spend each day in the profound awareness that
God does speak are in a wonderful position to receive his Word.

—Henry and Richard Blackaby

Willing to Wait

Habakkuk's conversation with God doesn't end here. There's a second exchange—the one that leads up to the climactic confirmation of the certainty of God's Word and its fulfillment. This second prayer shows us a man with his confidence restored. He still has his questions, sure—nothing wrong with that—but instead of wringing his hands, he's resting in expectation. Having taken time to observe God's handiwork with a new vision of what God is doing, he's no longer pointing a finger of blame at the heavens. He's certain now that God is indeed interested in what's going on, and he reaffirms his confidence in the power and fully present work of God.

> Are You not from everlasting, O Lord, my God, my
> Holy One? We will not die. You, O Lord, have appointed
> them to judge; and You, O Rock, have established them
> to correct. Your eyes are too pure to approve evil,
> and You cannot look on wickedness with favor.
> Habakkuk 1:12-13

Although worded as questions, the prophet's comments are really a declaration. Each inquiry demands an affirmative answer—an answer that confirms the prophet's restored confidence. They reveal that even though his problems and their details were largely unchanged, even though the surface map still wasn't looking much better than before, he had a new recognition and appreciation for God's position, power, and authority. He knew God was on the job. And with this acknowledgment of the magnitude of who he was dealing with, his level of expectancy grew. Even with circumstances still unchanged, he was no longer compelled to look down in loneliness and discouragement. His eyes were focused forward, eager to see what God's word and work would be next.

First, new vision.

Then, new confidence.

The result: a second wind to wait with.

> I will stand on my guard post and station myself on the
> rampart; and I will keep watch to see what He will speak
> to me and how I may reply when I am reproved. (2:1)

Habakkuk's posture is of someone who has a high expectation for a forthcoming work of God. The Hebrew words for "stand" and "station" are military terms. This man's composure was militant. His stance strong. His resolve sure. He was on the lookout, fully expecting God to answer.

And determined to wait until He did.

Habakkuk's use of this terminology reminds me of the guards outside London's Buckingham Palace. When we visited this past spring, our sons were enamored by these guys who refused to move no matter what happened. Tourists have been known to make faces at them and do all sorts of things to try distracting them, but they don't bat an eye or move a muscle. They know what they've been assigned to do, and they won't allow themselves to be diverted from their task, not even for a split second.

Even with the chaos of reality swirling around Habakkuk, God gave him so much confidence in who He was and what He could do that he was able to posture himself expectantly. If we value hearing from God as much as Habakkuk did, and if we are equally certain as he was that God will speak and that we will have the capacity to hear Him, we'll be determined to "stand" and "station" ourselves patiently. We'll be willing to wait. Always remember—*there is a direct correlation between our level of anticipation to hear from God and our willingness to wait.*

I've already admitted to you that waiting to hear from God is difficult for me. I imagine it probably is for you too. But I've learned this truth: the process of waiting for a message from Him is often just as important as the message itself. As I wait, my faith grows. The waiting prepares me to receive the message that's coming and to respond in obedience. In some cases, in fact, the intimacy I develop with my Father while I'm waiting *is* the message.

The waiting matters.

Have you ever been in a caravan, following in a line of cars that are all headed to the same destination? But instead of staying in position and trusting the lead car to steer you correctly, maybe you decided to go your own way, take a shortcut, or stop off for some coffee, thinking, "I can find the way there myself." Sure, it's happened to the best of us at one time or another. Instead of following patiently and awaiting the cues of the car in the lead, we've hopped ahead or gone off the course, assured that we could handle the drive ourselves. Often this hastiness and overly confident decision has led to one frustrating outcome: we were lost. Driving around for extra minutes, maybe even hours, we wished we'd stayed on course, trusted the person behind that lead wheel, and been patient enough to follow along. Refusing to do so cost us extra time, gas money, and emotional and mental energy. It seems that moving forward presumptuously often yields this outcome.

I wish I'd been prepared to wait before rushing into one decision I remember that really brought this point home to me. My friend Rachel had come to my house to show me a Bible study she'd been working on to help women make their home a sanctuary. It was very cool, very insightful—just like Rachel is—an interior decorator with not only great talent but a deep passion to share her gifts with others and bring glory to the Lord. She showed me the cover she'd designed for what she envisioned as a twelve-week Bible study, video series, journal, and gift booklet. Exciting stuff.

So when, after laying all of this material in front of me, she asked if I'd consider being her coauthor on the project, I jumped at the chance. Didn't even ask God what He thought about it. Right then and there, I told her I was in. She could count on me.

But after I had written the introductory chapters and sent them off to her, I knew I'd made a mistake. Through my personal Bible study and a clear, consistent impression from the Lord, He showed me that He wanted me focusing on something else at the time. My impulsive behavior had gotten me out of order. I'd put His will aside while plunging ahead with my own.

I'll never forget how ashamed I was to call Rachel after a couple months of hard work to tell her I couldn't partner with her on this after all.

And I could've saved myself that whole, sickening ordeal of inner turmoil and embarrassment if I would have simply sought the Lord's guidance and waited on His response before committing myself to the project. I could've kept from putting my friend in a bind and adversely affecting her plans for completing something that was rightly important to her. Gratefully, she was gracious and understanding, but I still felt awful about putting her in that situation.

The entire situation really spoke to something much deeper—an underlying doubt that He would speak to me about something so practical and personal, and that I could anticipate finding as much of His will in the waiting process as in His answer.

More than a few people have gotten married, moved to a different state, or made a major career change or financial decision before they took Habakkuk's example and waited patiently to hear from God, only to find out later that they would have been much better off if they had.

This, too, is where we must take a stand in our hearts. High above the ground-level realities we face every day, positioned where we can use our spiritual vision to take in the broad view from miles around, we gradually begin receiving a different perspective on our questions, decisions, and circumstances. Now we're watching only for God, trusting His lead, turning our attention completely to Him, not worried about what's happening below us or the speed with which our heart is telling us to react or respond. From this sturdy vantage point, with our priorities firmly fixed on hearing from God, waiting becomes something we're actually capable of doing.

Waiting expectantly becomes our normal.

Wouldn't that be something?

But this shouldn't really sound so far-fetched or seem so impossible. We *already* wait—all of us—for things that are important to us. We'll stay by the phone for hours waiting for a call about a job opportunity or a report from the doctor's office. We'll stand in line for groceries or a roller-coaster ride. We'll wait through the excitement-filled days and weeks before our wedding or the long months before our baby arrives. The value we place on something, the sense of anticipation we feel as it slowly, silently nears and makes its appearance, is in direct proportion to the amount of time we're willing to wait for it.

So as you have need, stand and wait.

His word is coming.

With complete confidence in Him, stand and wait, desiring Him and the sound of His voice more than anything.

He is coming.

Expect Him.

> If you want to hear God's voice clearly and you are uncertain, then remain in His presence until He changes this uncertainty. Often much can happen during this waiting on the Lord. Sometimes He changes pride into humility; doubt into faith and peace; sometimes lust into purity. The Lord can and will do it.
>
> —Corrie ten Boom

I'm Sure of It

With the prophet's stance changed from doubtful to confident, and his attitude from despondent to expectant, God began giving Habakkuk directions about what he should do. Remember, God's initial message had been designed to change the prophet's perspective and build his confidence. But this second time, He spoke to deliver specific instructions and guidance. It's almost as if God were saying, "Now that you have confidence and have come to Me expecting Me to answer you, let's get to it!"

And that's when God spoke to His beloved the encouraging promise recorded in Habakkuk 2:3—*the vision is coming.* "If it seems slow in coming, wait patiently, for it will surely take place. It will not be delayed" (NLT).

This is confirmation for us all. His word and its fulfillment will come to pass. You have His Word on it.

So expect more than you ever have—not because you now possess everything you need to know for every day moving forward. Not because God has given you clarity on what the next decade of your life will look like. Not because circumstances have suddenly smoothed over and you've no more need for His intervention. But expect because He has given you His promise.

And *that* . . . that is good enough.

"Behold, as the eyes of servants look to the hand of their master, as the eyes of a maid to the hand of her mistress, so our eyes look to the Lord our God, until He is gracious to us" (Psalm 123:2).

Can't wait to see what's next.

That's where God wants you to be—eagerly anticipating Him, moving as He moves, watching as He directs. He may lead you into challenge and difficulty. He may guide you smack-dab into a new opportunity and responsibility. Or He may open before you a season of rest, refreshment, and celebration. But those are only the details. The beauty of it all is that you're going there with Him, sure of His provision, tuned in to His larger purposes, and expecting more all the time from the One who blesses His children "according to the riches of His grace" (Ephesians 1:7).

That's why, when we get to the closing words of his book, we know exactly where Habakkuk's well-known benediction comes from. Now we can know the reason he could pray these closing words with such confidence, faith, and joy. Even with the adversity still on the horizon, the prophet could stand his ground and say . . .

> Though the fig tree should not blossom and there be no
> fruit on the vines, though the yield of the olive should fail
> and the fields produce no food, though the flock should be cut
> off from the fold and there be no cattle in the stalls, yet I will
> exult in the Lord, I will rejoice in the God of my salvation.
> Habakkuk 3:17–18

I don't know what has you on God's doorstep at this hour of the day or night—something relational, something financial, something tragic perhaps, something seemingly without any reason. I don't know what kinds of decisions you're facing in your family, in your work, in your health, in your future.

But I know this: Habakkuk's holy anticipation can be our own. Like admirable biblical characters of old, we don't have to call out to God and then walk away despondently. They called upon Him and . . .

He answered. He led. He counseled. He guided.

He speaks.

God speaks.

Your Lord and Savior speaks. To you.

So wake up expecting. Arrive expecting. Come expecting. Live expecting. Never stop . . .

Expecting.

From where He is—within you—to wherever you are, your God will speak persistently and personally, with both peace and challenge, in His truth and authority, to enable you to know and experience Him, to be an invited participant in His eternal plans for this age, and to see and feel firsthand the incomparable blessings of obedience.

This is His Word.

This is His promise.

Now, beloved . . . live like you believe it.

SOURCES OF QUOTES

Kay Arthur's quotes were given to the author.

Pat Ashley's quote was given to the author.

Henry Blackaby and Richard Blackaby, *Hearing God's Voice* (B&H Books, 2002).

Jill Briscoe's story in chapter 10 is from her book *Spiritual Arts: Mastering the Disciples for a Rich Spiritual Life* (Zondervan, 2007).

Lewis Sperry Chafer, *He That Is Spiritual: A Classic Doctrine of Spirituality* (Zondervan, 1983).

Oswald Chambers, *My Utmost for His Highest*.

Elisabeth Elliot, *On Asking God Why: Reflections on Trusting God* (Revell, 2006).

Matthew Henry (1662–1714) was an English clergyman who wrote commentaries on the Old and New Testaments.

Joyce Huggett, *The Joy of Listening to God* (IVP Books, 1987).

Jan Johnson, *When the Soul Listens: Finding Rest and Direction in Contemplative Prayer* (NavPress, 1999). Also see janjohnson.org.

Anne Graham Lotz, *Pursuing More of Jesus* (Thomas Nelson, 2009).

Peter Lord, *Hearing God* (Baker, 1988).

J. I. Packer, *Knowing God* (InterVarsity Press).

Hannah Whitall Smith, *The Christian's Secret to a Happy Life*, public domain.

Bob Sorge, *Secrets of the Secret Place* (Oasis House, 2009).

Corrie ten Boom, *Not I, but Christ* (Revell, 1997).

A. W. Tozer, *Man: The Dwelling Place of God* and *The Pursuit of God* (Wingspread Publishers).

Steve Verney, *Fire in Coventry* (Hodder and Stoughton, 1965).

Bruce Wilkinson, *Secrets of the Vine: Breaking through to Abundance* (Multnomah, 2006).

Philip Yancey's quote in chapter 3 was given to the author.

ACKNOWLEDGMENTS

*T*o my sons: Jackson, Jerry Jr. and Jude. Your childlike faith and quizzical interest in the things of God are the joy of my heart. Our conversations about spiritual things, egged on by your inquiries, before bed or while out running errands have been the most endearing part of being your mother. I hope you never stop seeking and searching for the things of God. Pursue Him. Hear Him. Follow Him. I love you.

At the first printing of this book, I acknowledged all four of my grandparents and wrote, "If you see the Lord first, tell Him that I'm coming." Since that time, my maternal grandfather has gone to heaven. He lived and died well. I'm certain when he met the Lord he heard a rousing, "Well done, faithful servant." I am grateful for his life and legacy and honored to still have three grandparents walking with me in the journey of life. Thank you all for your continued prayers, counsel, wisdom, and example of godliness.

A special thank-you to Lawrence; my friend and partner in writing. What a blessing it is to work with you. Thank you for helping me renovate and refresh this very important book.

Greg Thornton and my friends at Moody Publishers. Jerry and I have worked with you for nearly fifteen years now, and the privilege has been ours. Thank you for allowing this book the honor of wearing your imprint. Moody Publishers' legacy of faith and faithfulness is an incredibly important and valuable asset to this book and to our ministry. Thank you.

ABOUT THE AUTHOR

*P*riscilla Shirer is a wife and mom first, but put a Bible in her hand and a message in her heart, and you'll see why thousands meet God in powerful, personal ways at her conferences. She has authored several bestselling books and Bible studies including *One In A Million: Journey to Your Promised Land*; *Life Interrupted: Navigating the Unexpected*; *A Jewel In His Crown*; and *The Resolution For Women*. She and her husband, Jerry, lead Going Beyond Ministries from their hometown of Dallas, Texas, never too far from their three growing boys.

www.goingbeyond.com

Before you go . . .
share your thoughts with your friends

- Tweet/share that you finished *Discerning the Voice of God*
- Write a Review Amazon.com, CBD.com., BarnesandNoble.com, Moody Publishers.com
- Connect with Priscilla; follow her on Twitter @PriscillaShirer
- Learn about her ministry GoingBeyond.com
- Like Going Beyond on Facebook

MOODY
PUBLISHERS

www.MoodyPublishers.com

STANDARD DATA
RATES MAY APPLY

He Speaks to Me

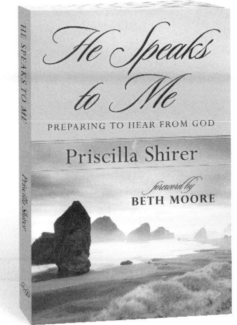

Do you want to develop a more intimate prayer life? Even more, do you want to hear from God in practical ways? Let Priscilla Shirer prepare you by giving you a deeper understanding of the Holy Spirit. Based on the life of Samuel, who first heard God's voice while still a small boy, this book is packed with practical examples from Priscilla's own life. *He Speaks to Me* addresses the need to develop a richer prayer life and deeper, more intimate relationship with God, and to learn how to comfortably share your experience of God with others.

MOODY
PUBLISHERS
www.MoodyPublishers.com

A Jewel in His Crown

ISBN-13: 978-0-8024-4083-9

ISBN-13: 978-0-8024-4094-5

Did you know that when you became a follower of Christ, you were born into a royal family? That you are a precious daughter of the King of all kings, destined for beauty, holiness, and victory?

A Jewel in His Crown speaks to women who in their weariness and discouragement have lost sight of their real value as beloved daughters of God. Through the Scriptures the book and workbook will help women rediscover their inestimable value to God as His beloved daughters and teach them how to renew their strength and be women of excellence.

MOODY
PUBLISHERS

www.MoodyPublishers.com

And We Are Changed

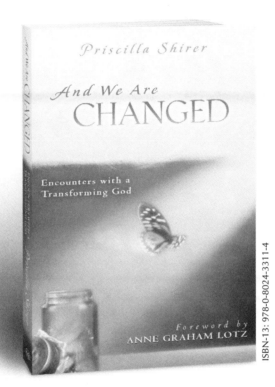

ISBN-13: 978-0-8024-3311-4

It is troubling how often we cease to be amazed at the transforming power of God in people's lives. When we meet Jesus, we are supposed to be changed. Jesus' death not only saves us and secures heaven for us, it is the power by which we can live a victorious Christian life here on earth. In *And We Are Changed*, Priscilla Shirer challenges readers to walk in freedom, throwing off the chains that have kept them from fully following Christ. She helps readers discover how to let the Word of God set us free, transforming us for His glory.

www.MoodyPublishers.com